Daily Dose of HISTORY

The Truth of History Through Stories, Quotes, & Trivia

JOSHUA YOHE

and

RYAN TROUTMAN

Authors: Joshua Yohe and Ryan Troutman
Contributors: Drew Stapleton and Micaiah Albert
Editors: Michala Archut and Katelyn Troutman
Cover design and layout: Caleb Sill

Printed in the United States of America

First Printing, 2019
ISBN 9781712276679
LCCN 2019919757

To Michala, thanks for supporting me in this endeavor
—Josh

To my amazing family, much appreciation for always supporting and encouraging my love for history
—Ryan

Citations for the Remarkable Remarks are at the end of the book.

INTRODUCTION

We have all received homespun advice before. Some of it is profound, some of it easily applicable, and some of it quirky, with a hint of the smart aleck:

Question: *How do you eat an elephant?*
Answer: *One bite at a time.*

You might have received this piece of armchair wisdom from a teacher that was helping you finish that insurmountable assignment, and it was likely that final term paper in history. Let's face it, history is full of these "insurmountables," these big chunks: big assignments, multi-volume works, the "collected papers." However, if you have been a student of history long enough, you have found another path to pursue your love of the past, and that is to study and learn about history a little bit at a time.

Where "learning a little until you know a lot" became a reality for me was when I was in college and one of my history teachers got us started learning about our family history. He gave us one of those mimeographed charts with the empty family tree on it, and we had to fill in the blanks with our ancestors' names. That chart took us back to our great, great grandparents, but I was able to fill in the chart completely—all sixteen of them—as I got my parents and my two grandmothers involved. That started for me a life-long pursuit of researching my family history, which has continued for over thirty years.

It was through genealogical research that I discovered that history comes in small doses. I might go for days without finding anything relevant while I was combing through census records, traipsing through a graveyard reading the headstones, spooling through microfilm at the county library, or reading the birth and death records in a family Bible. You even get used to going for long stretches without finding much, but you stay at it anyway because, well. . . you might discover another piece that fits with your story. I found out that as I plugged away, I had incrementally compiled a unique history of my family that had not previously been compiled.

Josh Yohe and Ryan Troutman have written a book that reminds us that history takes place every moment and that it is made up of various types of events. Some events are grand and consequential, like the creation of the UN; some tragic, like the explosion of the Space Shuttle *Challenger*; and some even bizarre, like the CIA toying with the idea of filling Castro's cigars with explosives, or Reagan's fascination with "little green men" from space. Josh and Ryan have done this by telling us simple stories, simply stated. To coin a phrase, he has not overburdened us with "ostentatious erudition."

Josh and Ryan also remind us that history is not just a subject; it's a regular occurrence. For the serious student of history, for those of us that have found history "habit forming," we work to approach it often. Josh and Ryan have provided us the opportunity to approach it daily, "line upon line, precept upon precept…"

One bite at a time…

—William R. Bowen, Jr., Ph.D
New Bern, North Carolina

THE COLD WAR

As World War II (WWII) came to a close, the United States was the only major superpower able to stop the drive of the Soviet Union. As the two powers faced off, the idea of another world war and nuclear annihilation kept them from an all-out war. Instead, they turned to spying, subterfuge, weapons buildup, and stealing each other's technological secrets. They also fought either overtly or secretly in proxy wars and conflicts across the globe.

As this Cold War (war of words without open fighting) took place from 1945 to 1991, the United States seemingly only became more powerful, while their rival the Soviet Union became weaker. The Space Race, arms race, nuclear race, and even sports rivalries all influenced both countries and the world throughout the Cold War. Ultimately, the democracy of the United States defeated the Communism of the Soviet Union, and the entire world moved on into the global age.

THE WORLD WE LIVE IN

Remarkable Remark

"[Following WWII] Newly independent nations emerged into what has now become known as the Third World. Their role in world affairs is becoming increasingly significant."
—*President Jimmy Carter*

Exciting Entry

On this day in 1895, John Edgar Hoover was born. One of the most iconic and powerful Americans for nearly 50 years, Hoover led the FBI in criminal, communist, and other subversive investigations.

Prominent Passing

On this day in 1992, Grace Hopper died. A relatively unknown mathematician and naval officer, she pioneered many advances in the computer industry and earned several awards for her lifetime of work.

With the end of WWII, the United States and the USSR began forming alliances with other nations in an effort to protect their ideals. This effort led to the terms First, Second, and Third World countries. Many today use these terms without realizing the origin of the terms they are using.

While in today's terminology First, Second, and Third World tend to refer to a country's economic development, during the Cold War, it referred to a country's political alignment.

First World countries consisted of any country that aligned with the United States and the ideals of freedom and a capitalistic economy. NATO members, Japan, Australia, and others typically made up the First World throughout the Cold War.

Second World countries were any country that aligned, or were forced to align, with the ideals of the Communist Soviet Union. These countries mainly consisted of Eastern European nations, China, and other Asian nations. Following the collapse of the Soviet Union, the term Second World generally fell out of use.

Third World countries during the Cold War consisted of any nation not aligned with either the United States or the Soviet Union. The majority of Central and South America, Africa, and the Middle East fell into this category. Many of these nations were fought over by both First and Second World countries in an effort to instill their ideals into those countries.

FORMATION OF THE UN

The United Nations officially came into existence on October 24, 1945, after being ratified by each of its main members and many of the smaller ones. However, both the idea and the name of the United Nations had been around for quite some time before that day in October.

The idea of a one-world government, that could resolve conflicts through negotiation instead of war, dates back to at least World War I. The League of Nations was supposed to keep the peace following the "War to End All Wars" and yet did nothing to stop Hitler, Mussolini, or Japanese militarists. Many blame the failure of the League of Nations on the United States because Congress refused to allow the country to join.

The actual name "United Nations" dates back to 1942. On January 1, 1942, President Franklin Delano Roosevelt delivered the Declaration by United Nations, which declared the intent of twenty-six countries to continue fighting the Axis Powers.

The UN claims to provide humanitarian aid, maintain global peace and security, protect the basic human rights of all people, and many other noble endeavors. Whether the United Nations is actually effective is a story for another day, as over 150 wars have been fought since its founding.

Remarkable Remark

"WE THE PEOPLES OF THE UNITED NATIONS [ARE] DETERMINED to save succeeding generations from the scourge of war, which twice in our life- time has brought untold sorrow to mankind."
—*UN Charter*

Exciting Entry

On this day in 1954, Lyudmila Vasilyevna Borozna was born. A volleyball player for the Soviet Union, she and her team won gold at the 1972 summer Olympics in Munich, West Germany.

Prominent Passing

On this day in 2001, William Pierce Rogers died. Rogers was the US attorney general under the Eisenhower Administration and the secretary of state during President Nixon's administration.

THE COLD WAR

Exciting Entry

On this day in 1883,
Clement Attlee was
born. He became prime
minister of Great Britain
at the end of WWII, led
England through the first
few years of the Cold
War, and helped India
gain independence.

Prominent Passing

On this day in 2015, Ed-
ward William Brooke III
died. In 1966, he became
the first black man to be
popularly elected to the
US Senate and was one
of the first to call for President Nixon's resignation.

With the end of WWII, the two remaining superpowers, the United States and the Soviet Union, began a new war of words and ideologies. This "war" was coined a "Cold War" by two men at the very beginning of the decades-long conflict.

The first person to use the term *Cold War* was the English author George Orwell, whose best-known works are *Animal Farm* and *1984*. Orwell wrote an essay in 1945 entitled "You and the Atom Bomb," in which he referred to a *Cold War*. However, Orwell's use of the term did not yet take hold in the world stage, and it was another two years before the term became popular.

In 1947, Bernard Baruch was giving a speech during a ceremony honoring him when he used the term *Cold War*. Baruch was a millionaire, financier, and presidential advisor for nearly every president from Woodrow Wilson to Lyndon B. Johnson. Baruch used the phrase during an impassioned speech, written by his close friend and confidant, Herbert Bayard Swope. It was this use of Cold War that popularized the term, and soon everyone was referring to the time of conflict as the Cold War.

The Cold War was in itself a unique war, as no overt fighting was done between the United States and the USSR. Instead, espionage, subversion, and "proxy" wars like the Korean and Vietnam Wars became popular. The Cold War ended with the fall of the Soviet Union and led to the rise of the global age.

THE THING

During the Cold War, espionage played a key role in each side's attempting to take the lead, and each side tried many unique ways at gaining the other side's secrets.

In August of 1945, a group of Soviet students presented the US ambassador a carved Great Seal of the United States as a token of appreciation for being their WWII ally. However, this sign of friendship was actually a Soviet listening device that wasn't discovered until three ambassadors later, in 1952.

This listening device didn't contain its own power source and was instead controlled by a strong radio signal. In 1951, a British radio operator picked up the bug, but a search of the embassy proved futile. Again in 1952, an American interceptor overheard a conversation, and a thorough sweep and investigation turned up a listening device embedded in the carving behind the ambassador's desk.

The United States didn't reveal that they knew about the bug until the 1960 Gary Powers incident, when they used it to prove that spying between the two countries was mutual. It was nicknamed "The Thing" or "The Great Seal Bug." During the Cold War, other Soviet bugs were found in different US embassies, but both countries continued to spy on the other one. Espionage led to advancements by both the United States and the USSR; however, it only provided another avenue for strained relations between the two countries during the Cold War.

Remarkable Remark

"We had long since taught ourselves to assume that in Moscow most walls—at least in rooms that diplomats were apt to frequent—had ears."
—*George Kennan*

Exciting Entry

On this day in 1904, John Alex McCone was born. He was the director of the Central Intelligence Agency (CIA) during the Cuban Missile Crisis, JFK's assassination, and part of the Vietnam War.

Prominent Passing

On this day in 2004, John Toland died. Toland wrote several groundbreaking books on WWII, including books on Hitler and the Japanese Empire and won the Pulitzer Prize in 1971 for nonfiction.

Jan **5**

NATO FORMED

Exciting Entry
On this day in 1876, Kon-rad Adenauer was born. An anticommunist, he was the first chancel-lor of West Germany and worked to rebuild his country's econo-my and relationships with other countries.

Prominent Passing
On this day in 2007, Mo-mofuku Ando died. Fol-lowing WWII, he created a quickly prepared meal for the war-torn country of Japan to eat. Today, people eat his creation, instant ramen, worldwide.

In 1949, the United States and many western European countries joined the North Atlantic Treaty Organization, commonly referred to as NATO. Today, NATO is often referenced by the president; however, few know what this organization is.

The North Atlantic Treaty Organization was originally formed to counter the threat of Soviet invasion of Western Europe. NATO's mandate is to provide a common defense for the European and Atlantic areas and to address common issues faced by the member countries. Article One of the treaty took pains to respect and complement the principles of the United Nations charter, which was signed four years earlier.

NATO is composed of a political and a military structure. The political component is based in Brussels, Belgium, where the North Atlantic Council (NAC) makes all political decisions. Defense ministers or heads of state may represent their nations depending on the importance of the issue at hand. Decisions are made on the basis of a consensus within the member nations. Militarily, a committee consisting of military representatives from the member states advises the NAC. NATO's military forces are also composed of forces voluntarily made available by the member states, and each state provides a certain percentage of monetary support. Today, NATO is used for continued military partnership.

Jan **6** CHURCHILL'S IRON CURTAIN

On March 5, 1946, one of the most iconic lines of the Cold War was delivered in Fulton, Missouri, by British statesman Winston Churchill.

Joined by President Harry S. Truman on stage, Winston Churchill delivered the line that emphasized the term *Iron Curtain*. In his speech, Churchill was referencing the expansionist policies and practices of the Soviet Union. For his comments, Churchill was labeled a racist by the Soviets.

Just one year earlier, Churchill had surprisingly lost his re-election bid for prime minister of Britain. This stunning defeat came after he led his country back from the brink of collapse against the Nazi blitzkrieg all the way to the doorstep of Berlin.

In honor of his achievements, Winston Churchill was the first person to receive honorary citizenship of the United States. One common misconception is that the Marquis de Lafayette was the first to receive honorary American citizenship. In the eighteenth century, several individual colonies awarded Lafayette and his heirs the honor of being a "citizen," but it was not awarded by the US Congress or the president. In 2002, Lafayette was awarded "citizenship" posthumously. Regardless of when and who received an honorary US citizenship, both Winston Churchill and Lafayette were deserving of the honor.

Remarkable Remark
"From Stettin in the Baltic to Trieste in the Adriatic, an iron curtain has descended across the Continent. Behind that line lie all the capitals of the ancient [European] states."
— *Winston Churchill*

Exciting Entry
On this day in 1912, Danny Thomas was born. A TV star, his greatest influence came in 1962, when he founded the South's first fully integrated children's hospital, St. Jude Children's Research Hospital.

Prominent Passing
On this day in 2006, Hugh Thompson Jr. died. Serving in the Vietnam War, he was one of the men who rescued Vietnamese during the Mai Lai massacre and testified before Congress about the event.

Jan 7 — COMMUNIST JOKES

Remarkable Remark

"A man goes into a shop and asks "You don't have any meat?" "No, replied the sales lady, "We don't have any fish. It's the store across the street that doesn't have any meat."
— *Joke about Soviets told by CIA*

Exciting Entry

On this day in 1926, Kim Jong-pil was born. A South Korean politician, Jong-pil helped presidents rise to power, created their infamous intelligence agency, and shaped their foreign policy for decades.

Prominent Passing

On this day in 1989, Hirohito died. Emperor during WWII, Hirohito was the first Japanese monarch to visit a foreign country while reigning when he visited Europe and the United States during the 1970s.

During the Cold War, both the Soviets and the Americans made fun of the other. However, the CIA compiled a number of political jokes that the Soviets told each other, making fun of their own country. The CIA declassified these jokes, and some of the best are below as originally written.

1) A worker standing in a liquor line says, "I have had enough, save my place, I am going to shoot Gorbachev." Two hours later he returns to claim his place in line. His friends ask, "Did you get him?" No, the line there was even longer than the line here.

2) Sentence from a schoolboy's weekly composition class essay – "My cat just had seven kittens. They are all communists." Sentence from the same boy's composition the following week – "My cat's seven kittens are all capitalist." Teacher reminds boy that the previous week he had said the kittens were communists. "But now they've opened their eyes," replies the child.

3) A joke heard in Arkhangelsk has it that someone happened to call the KGB headquarters just after a major fire. "We cannot do anything. The KGB has just burned down" he was told. Five minutes later he called back and was told again that the KGB had burned. When he called a third time, the telephone operator recognized his voice and asked, "Why do you keep calling back? I just told you, the KGB has burned down." "I know," the man replied. "I just like to hear it."

Jan **8**

"UNDER GOD"

Since Francis Bellamy penned the words to the Pledge of Allegiance in 1892, schoolchildren and adults across the United States have recited it. However, it was not until 1954 that the words "under God" were added to the pledge.

Originally written to celebrate the Columbian Exposition in 1892, Bellamy's original pledge stated, "I pledge allegiance to my flag and to the Republic for which it stands—one Nation indivisible—with liberty and justice for all." However, in the 1920s, the phrase "to my flag" was changed to "the flag of the United States of America" so that immigrants would clearly understand to which country they were pledging their allegiance.

During this same period, many of the children saluted the flag with a salute that resembled Hitler's own salute. It was because of Hitler's Nazi salute and the atrocities committed by Hitler's regime that people now place their right hand over their heart when saying the pledge. In 1942, the pledge was made a part of the national flag code.

Remarkable Remark
"I pledge allegiance to the Flag of the United States of America, and to the Republic for which it stands, one Nation under God, indivisible, with liberty and justice for all."
—*Pledge of Allegiance*

Exciting Entry
On this day in 1902, Georgy Malenkov was born. A powerful Communist party member, Malenkov was a close comrade of Joseph Stalin and became prime minister of the Soviet Union following Stalin's death.

Prominent Passing
On this day in 1976, Zhou Enlai died. A powerful Chinese Communist, Enlai worked alongside Mao Zedong and others to implement many of the Communist social and economic reforms throughout China.

In 1952, the Knights of Columbus began lobbying for the words "under God" to be added to the pledge. In 1954, President Dwight D. Eisenhower signed a law adding the words "under God" to the pledge in an effort to signify America's godly morality which was in contrast to the atheistic communist mentality of the Soviet Union.

KOREAN WAR (1950-1953)

Remarkable Remark

"The Communist threat is a global one...You cannot appease or otherwise surrender to communism in Asia without simultaneously undermining our efforts to halt its advance in Europe."

—MacArthur

Exciting Entry

On this day in 1913, Richard Milhous Nixon was born. A career politician, Nixon won the presidential election of 1968; however, he resigned in 1974 because of his role in the Watergate Scandal.

Prominent Passing

On this day in 1966, Albert Stevens died. He was given plutonium because of a misdiagnosis and absorbed the largest accumulated dose of plutonium any human has ever received, though never consenting.

Following WWII, the Korean Peninsula was divided along the 38th Parallel. North Korea was set up with a Communist government, while South Korea set up a democratic-style government. The fragile peace ended when North Korea invaded South Korea.

Quickly overrun, the South Koreans were pushed almost all the way into the sea at Pusan. There, General Douglas MacArthur assumed command of the American and their allies' forces. To relieve the pressure at the Pusan Perimeter, MacArthur ordered a daring assault at Inchon, a Communist-held city that was lightly defended. This victory cut off the supply lines of the Communist Korean People's Army (KPA).

The Americans and their allies proceeded to crush the Communists, then marched past the 38th Parallel, pursuing the retreating KPA soldiers all the way to the northern regions of North Korea. Communist China sent in an army to assist the North Koreans, slowly pushing MacArthur back.

MacArthur wanted to wage a total war against China, but was opposed by President Truman who eventually fired him. MacArthur was replaced by Matthew Ridgway, who had been commanding the ground forces. Only when Truman was succeeded by Dwight Eisenhower was an armistice actually signed, bringing the conflict to an unsatisfactory close.

USPS ROCKET MAIL

During the Cold War, many unbelievable inventions were created. With the dawn of the space age, the United States began experimenting with rockets in many avenues of life. One of those avenues was with the mail.

The Post Office Department (now called the USPS) considered using rockets to deliver mail, both domestically and internationally. In 1959, Postmaster General Arthur Summerfield predicted that rocket mail would be the future of mail delivery.

The only time that mail delivery by rocket occurred successfully was in June of 1959, when the submarine USS *Barbero* launched a rocket filled with 3,000 pieces of mail toward Florida. The missile was fired around noon and reached its destination twenty-two minutes later. The mail was then sorted and routed as the typical mail was.

The Post Office Department set up a post office on the submarine, and the mail was given a USS *Barbero* postal mark. It is interesting to note that each letter was written by Summerfield and said the same thing. The letters were sent to postmasters around the globe, to the submarine crew, and even to President Dwight D. Eisenhower. While using missiles quickened mail delivery, it also showed the world how accurate the United States' missiles were. This futuristic mail delivery system never "took off," and today, thousands of USPS workers continue to deliver the mail by car, train, and airplane.

Remarkable Remark

"In my judgment, before man reaches the moon, your mail will be delivered within hours from New York to California, to England, to India, or to Australia by guided missiles."
—*Arthur Summerfield*

Exciting Entry

On this day in 1913, Gustav Husak was born. A communist for most of his life, he rose through the ranks to become the Communist Party president of Czechoslovakia for roughly two decades.

Prominent Passing

On this day in 1980, George Meany died. Meany merged the two largest labor organizations in the United States and led the newly formed AFL-CIO as president throughout much of the Cold War.

CIA PLOTS TO KILL CASTRO

Remarkable Remark

"If there were an Olympic event in this field [surviving assassination attempts], I would certainly have won the gold medal."

—Fidel Castro

Exciting Entry

On this day in 1903, Alan Stewart Paton was born. Paton was the author of *Cry, the Beloved Country* which brought international attention to the issue of apartheid that was occurring in South Africa.

Prominent Passing

On this day in 2008, Sir Edmund Percival Hillary died. Hillary was a mountain climber, who along with Tenzing Norgay, became the first people to reach the summit of Mount Everest which they did in 1953.

Following the ascension of Fidel Castro in 1959, the US government and especially the CIA, looked for ways to kill Castro. While none were successful, it is estimated by Cuban officials that Castro survived over 630 different attempts on his life, many of which were attempted by the CIA.

Knowing Castro's love for cigars, the CIA thought of filling a cigar with explosives when he attended an UN meeting, but it never happened. The CIA recruited a double agent to give Castro a botulin-filled cigar that would kill him. The CIA also wanted to put a chemical in Castro's cigar in an attempt to make him disoriented prior to a speech.

The CIA also tried to exploit his love for scuba diving by placing a conch shell with an explosive device near his favorite diving spot. They also thought of sending him a wetsuit lined with bacteria that could cause a skin disease.

The CIA even hired the Mafia and used a sharpshooter to kill Castro. In 2000, explosives were going to be used in Panama under the stage where Castro was giving a speech. The CIA also considered using a pen with a poisoned-filled hypodermic needle so fine, that Castro would not notice when someone bumped into him. While it is uncertain the exact number of assassination attempts Castro survived, he did survive the many unique attempts the CIA thought up and occasionally attempted.

FRANCIS GARY POWERS

During the Cold War, the United States and the Soviet Union tried many different ways to spy on the other. One of the ways the United States tried to spy on the Soviet Union was with their U-2 spy plane.

However, after several successful espionage missions, the Soviets shot down a CIA U-2 spy plane on May 1, 1960, and captured the pilot, Francis Gary Powers. The United States, believing the plane destroyed and pilot dead, denied that it was a spy plane, claiming that it was instead a weather plane. The Soviet Union proved otherwise, leaving the US government in an awkward position.

On May 16, Nikita Khrushchev met in Paris with Dwight D. Eisenhower and was furious about the incident. Khrushchev wasted no time in tearing into the United States, declaring that President Eisenhower would not be welcome in Russia during his scheduled visit to the Soviet Union in June, ending the current summit with the US president because of the US espionage venture.

Powers was released two years later in exchange for a captured senior Soviet KGB colonel. Ironically, when the Soviet Union went to the UN to condemn the United States for their espionage, the United States revealed "The Thing" in response and proved that Cold War espionage was mutual between both powers. The UN did not condemn the United States and both countries continued spying on each other.

Remarkable Remark

"Comrades, I must tell you a secret: When I was making my report I deliberately did not say that the pilot was alive and in good health and that we have parts of the plane."
—*Nikita Khrushchev*

Exciting Entry

On this day in 1917, Maharishi Mahesh Yogi was born. He was a Hindu religious leader who popularized the practice of transcendental meditation in the West and gained many celebrity followers.

Prominent Passing

On this day in 2001, William Hewlett died. He cofounded Hewlett-Packard Company which became prominent during the Cold War for its calculators, printers, and other technological advancements.

BAY OF PIGS

Exciting Entry

On this day in 1906, Zhou Youguang was born. He created the Pinyin system of Chinese writing which helped raise Chinese literacy rates nearly 70 percent. He is remembered as the "Father of Pinyin."

Prominent Passing

On this day in 1978, Hubert Humphrey Jr. died. Humphrey served as President Lyndon B. Johnson's vice president and was an unsuccessful presidential candidate in 1968, losing to Richard Nixon.

During the Cold War, the United States and the Soviet Union were involved in several "proxy wars" and major incidents. One of these major incidents occurred in 1961 in Cuba.

Following the rise of Cuban dictator Fidel Castro in 1959, the next major Cuban incident occurred in 1961, when the Bay of Pigs invasion began. Originally the brainchild of President Eisenhower, it was President Kennedy that put the plan into operation. Supposedly a secret operation, Castro knew of the plan by October of 1960, and even US newspapers reported on the proposed invasion, infuriating President Kennedy.

On April 17, 1961, the Cuban-exile invasion force, Brigade 2506, landed at beaches along the Bay of Pigs and immediately came under heavy fire. President Kennedy ordered an "air-umbrella" at dawn on April 19, but the B-26s arrived an hour late and were shot down by the Cubans. The invasion was crushed later that day, with many of the members of the invasion forces being captured.

On December 23, 1962, a plane containing the first group of freed prisoners landed in the United States. Determined to make up for the failed invasion, Kennedy initiated Operation Mongoose—a plan which included the possibility of assassinating Castro. The Bay of Pigs was one of JFK's biggest blunders and set Soviet-US relations further apart.

DAILY LIFE IN THE COLD WAR

On July 16, 1929, in Oaklyn, New Jersey, Louis and Mabel Archut had a son named Lewis (Lew) Archut. During WWII, Lew was in high school, and he graduated in 1948. While in high school, Lew worked at a grocery store and a gas station. After graduation, he skipped college to learn a trade and eventually worked for Rohm and Haas in Philadelphia from 1948 to 1991.

In 1949, Lew went on a blind date and met Marie Enders, a nursing student in Barrington, NJ. They dated for a couple years, and on June 14, 1952, Lew and Marie were married. They had two children and were married for fifty-seven years until Marie's passing in 2008.

During Lew's time in New Jersey, he and some others started and built their own church. They built it in the weekday evenings and on Saturdays. When they ran out of money for their building project, they held a prayer meeting for funds to continue building. The church they built is still there holding services today, Community Bible Church of Barrington, NJ.

In 1993, Lew moved after retirement to South Carolina for his wife's health, to be closer to family, and for the cheaper cost of living. He continued his hobbies such as fishing, oil painting, and watching his lifelong favorite team, the Philadelphia Eagles. His life, while seemingly normal, is one that the average American during the Cold War would have lived: going to church, working, and supporting his family.

Remarkable Remark

"Lewis Archut isn't afraid to speak the truth or say what needs to be said. He loved his wife and provided for his family. He is a wise man, and I'm proud to call him my grandfather."
—*Michala Archut*

Exciting Entry

On this day in 1905, Takeo Fukuda was born. He served as Japan's prime minister in the late 1970s and issued the Fukuda Doctrine that stated that Japan would never again become a military power.

Prominent Passing

On this day in 1977, Anthony Eden died. He served as Great Britain's prime minister in 1955 and welcomed Soviet leader Nikita Khrushchev to Great Britain in an effort to ease Cold War tensions.

COLD WAR TREATIES

Exciting Entry
On this day in 1880, Ibn Saud was born. Under his leadership Saudi Arabia was formed in the 1930s, and during the Cold War, the oil-rich kingdom became a leading exporter of oil throughout the world.

Prominent Passing
On this day in 1988, Seán Macbride died. He helped found Amnesty International and worked with the International Peace Bureau. He won the Nobel Peace Prize for his human rights efforts in 1974.

During the Cold War, neither the United States nor the Soviet Union wanted the other one to gain an upper hand. To that end, both made treaties and agreements with the other to neutralize the potential for conflict.

Antarctica, while mostly uninhabitable, was claimed by many nations following WWII. However, in 1959, the United States, USSR, and many other nations agreed to only use Antarctica for scientific purposes to prevent a weapons buildup there in the Cold War.

In 1967, as the space race began escalated, the potential for nuclear weapons in space began to worry many on both sides of the conflict. To quell these concerns, the United States, USSR, and other nations all agreed to use space only for peaceful purposes and prohibited nuclear weapons in space or on the Moon.

Perhaps the most unusual agreement between the United States and the USSR came in 1985 during the Geneva Summit. President Ronald Reagan and Soviet Premier Mikhail Gorbachev had temporarily stopped the talks and took a private walk together with only an interpreter. For many years, it was unknown what they discussed; however, in 2009, Gorbachev revealed that the two had agreed to stop hostilities if the earth was invaded by aliens! While the numerous treaties signed during the Cold War did little to limit the threat of war, many of the treaties signed and agreements made are still in effect today.

Jan 16 — SIX DAYS' WAR

On June 5, 1967, Israel launched a pre-emptive strike against the Arab military buildup on their border, sparking six days of intense warfare.

The surprise attack on the Egyptian air force was successful, wiping out half of Egypt's planes, despite a warning being sent by a Jordanian radar facility. The Israeli pilots were tired after being in battle for about twenty-four hours, yet the Arabs did not take advantage.

Israeli ground troops pressed down toward Sinai and found outpost after outpost that had been deserted by the Egyptians, some with all of the supplies left behind. By day three of the war, political pressure was mounting on Israel to accept a ceasefire proposed by King Hussein of Jordan. At the last moment, the ceasefire was scrapped because of King Hussein's unwillingness to comply with his own terms. The delay allowed the Israelis to capture the Old City of Jerusalem and bring it under their control. They continued to retake cities and landmarks of historical and spiritual significance, such as the city of Hebron.

Remarkable Remark
"I have just come from Jerusalem to tell the Security Council [of the UN] that Israel, by its independent effort and sacrifice, has passed from serious danger to successful resistance."
—Abba Eban

Exciting Entry
On this day in 1901, Fulgencio Batista was born. Cuban dictator for several years, he was ousted by Fidel Castro in the 1950s, resulting in Cuba's becoming a Communist country and threat to the United States.

Prominent Passing
On this day in 2013, Pauline Phillips died. Known professionally as Abigail Van Buren or "Dear Abby," her column advised readers throughout the Cold War and beyond with its witty sayings.

On day five, an Israeli platoon of twenty-five men overran one of the most heavily fortified Syrian positions. The Syrians pulled out of the Golan Heights overnight; an attack could have cost the Israelis an estimated 30,000 lives on day six of fighting. A ceasefire was signed later that day.

APOLLO 8

Apollo 8 made history in several ways. It was the first spacecraft to carry man out of low Earth orbit and the first one to reach the Moon, orbit it, and return safely. It launched on December 21, 1968, and took sixty-eight hours to get to the Moon. In the span of twenty-four hours, they orbited the Moon ten times. It was during this period that the crew members made even more history. It was during these orbits that the Apollo crew made some more history, history in the form of a message.

The astronauts oversaw the content of the message that would be delivered but could not decide on what they wanted to say. After the astronauts asked around, Christine Laitin, the wife of a public affairs officer for President Johnson, gave them the idea to read Genesis 1.

Using a King James Version Bible that had been provided by the Gideons, the three astronauts Bill Anders, Jim Lovell, and Frank Borman took turns reading the first ten verses of Genesis 1.

The official transcript of the broadcast reads, "We are now approaching lunar sunrise, and for all the people back on Earth, the crew of Apollo 8 has a message that we would like to send to you." Anders read the first four verses, Lovell read the next four, and Borman finished with the last two verses. The transmission ended with the crew wishing the people on earth a Merry Christmas.

USS PUEBLO

During the Cold War, the American military had many highs and lows. One of the lows was the capture of the USS *Pueblo*, the only commissioned US naval vessel held by a foreign power.

On January 23, 1968, North Korea captured the USS *Pueblo*, a US spy vessel. In the attack, one American sailor was killed, and the eighty-two others were imprisoned and tortured for nearly a full year. According to the United States, the vessel was well in international waters when the North Koreans engaged the vessel. Many soldiers signed "confessions" after extreme torture.

A major incident then, it is often overlooked today because of the Tet Offensive in the Vietnam War starting a week later. Used as a propaganda item in North Korea to show the weakness of the United States, the vessel is viewed daily by North Koreans to prove their supremacy over the United States.

Exactly eleven months after the *Pueblo*'s capture, negotiators reached a settlement to resolve the crisis. Under the settlement's terms, the United States admitted the ship's intrusion into North Korean territory, apologized for the action, and pledged to cease any future such action. Afterwards, the United States denied intrusion into Korean waters, but the damage had already been done. The surviving crewmen walked one by one across the "Bridge of No Return" to freedom in South Korea. They were hailed as heroes and returned home to the United States in time for Christmas.

Remarkable Remark

"In spite of their hardships, every member of the crew remained faithful to the United States and kept faith with each other throughout their captivity."
—*Vice Admiral J.M. Boorda*

Exciting Entry

On this day in 1904, Archibald Leach was born. Known worldwide as Cary Grant, his acting led him to have a large following. He had a great appeal with the women because of his accent and style.

Prominent Passing

On this day in 1996, Rudolph Wanderone Jr. died. A well-known billiards player he used the nickname "Minnesota Fats" which reflected his large frame. He helped popularize billiards in the 1960s.

FIRST MAN ON THE MOON

Exciting Entry

On this day in 1920, Javier Pérez de Cuéllar was born. A Peruvian diplomat, he served from 1982 to 1991 as the secretary-general of the United Nations and later became Peru's prime minister.

Prominent Passing

On this day in 1921, Anatoly Bannik died. Bannik was a multi-winning chess champion in Ukraine and was a prominent player in the Soviet Union for nearly two decades during the Cold War.

During the Cold War, one of the major events was the space race. As both sides vied for power and a key accomplishment in space, the United States did not truly gain the lead in the space race until Apollo 11.

In 1961, President Kennedy made it a priority to land a man on the Moon by the end of the decade. While Kennedy did not live long enough to see his goal accomplished, it was achieved.

On July 16, 1969, Neil Armstrong, Edwin "Buzz" Aldrin, and Michael Collins took off from Florida on their way to the moon. On July 20, while Collins piloted the command module *Columbia*, Armstrong and Aldrin used the lunar module *Eagle* to descend onto the Moon.

Following the *Eagle's* touching down on the Moon, the two astronauts began preparing for walking on the Moon. Interestingly, the first item on the Moon was a duffle bag of trash tossed from the lunar module. It was following this that Neil Armstrong and later Buzz Aldrin walked on the moon and began exploring. The two astronauts stayed on the moon for nearly a day taking photographs, collecting rock samples, and conducting scientific experiments. The trio splashed down in the Pacific on July 24. The trio was debriefed on their mission and placed in quarantine for several days. Following this, they toured across the country and received numerous accolades and awards for their achievements.

 **VIETNAM WAR**

The Vietnam War is one of the most divisive topics in US history and is typically regarded as the first war the United States lost.

Vietnam had been under French rule since the 1860s. However, the Japanese invaded during WWII, leading to Ho Chi Minh's rise to power in Vietnam. He desired to fight off both the Japanese invaders and the French colonial administrators and ultimately became the communist president of the Democratic Republic of Vietnam (DRV) in North Vietnam.

Ngo Dinh Diem became president of South Vietnam and was backed by the United States. However, violence by both sides led to the beginning of conflict. In 1964, two US destroyers were attacked in the Gulf of Tonkin, leading to increased American presence in Vietnam.

The war was not popular with many Americans, leading to riots and protests. The media played an important role in informing and sometimes misleading the American people. The North Viatnamese led Tet Offensive stunned the United States and its allies, leading to a request for additional troops on the ground. However, President Nixon used the policy of Vietnamization. In this policy, the United States would provide the money, weapons, and other supplies, while the South Vietnamese would man them. In 1973, the United States and North Vietnam reached a final peace agreement. Just two years later, DRV forces captured Saigon and renamed it Ho Chi Minh City.

Remarkable Remark
"Let us be united for peace. Let us also be united against defeat. Because let us understand: North Vietnam cannot defeat or humiliate the United States. Only Americans can do that."
—*Richard Nixon*

Exciting Entry
On this day in 1930, Edwin "Buzz" Aldrin was born. Aldrin served in the US Air Force for several years before training to be an astronaut. He is best remembered as being the second man on the Moon.

Prominent Passing
On this day in 1993, Audrey Ruston died. Known as Audrey Hepburn, she starred in several movies including *Breakfast at Tiffany's*. In her later life, she conducted humanitarian work across the globe.

OPERATION CHROME DOME

Operation Chrome Dome, which lasted from 1960 until 1968, was a US Air Force mission which saw B-52 Stratofortress aircraft fly near the Soviet Union border while armed with thermonuclear weapons.

This Cold War-era mission was not without its fair share of mishaps. In January of 1966, one of the planes attempted to refuel in the air with a Boeing KC-135 Stratotanker, which is a military refueling aircraft. Unfortunately, the bomber was too fast, and a collision caused the left wing of the bomber to snap off.

In its deathly plummet, four nuclear weapons were released from the bomber. Three of those fell in the same general vicinity of the B-52 wreckage, which was located near the village of Palomares, Spain. One bomb was found near the Mediterranean beach, another in a tomato field, and the third in a cemetery. The fourth bomb was nowhere to be found. After eleven weeks of searching by more than thirty ships, the fourth bomb was located in the sea.

It took more than 1,600 US Air Force personnel to clean up the mess in Palomares, and the coverup of the event poorly executed. Tons of radioactive dirt had to be hauled away and many people were exposed to serious levels of plutonium. There were several more accidents involving nuclear weapons, but the worst of them occurred in Operation Chrome Dome.

CULTURAL REVOLUTIONS

During the Cold War, there were two major Cultural Revolutions in the world. The first was in Communist China and the second in the United States.

From 1966 to 1976, China underwent their Cultural Revolution under Mao Zedong. This revolution was his effort to gain more power within China. Zedong called on the Chinese youth to eliminate those in China who were untrue to Communism. Everyone from party leaders to the poor were killed. The Cultural Revolution left millions dead, injured, and imprisoned; and it took China years to recover.

In the United States, the Cultural Revolution occurred during the 1960s-1970s. By the 1960s, the American youth were tired of traditional ideals such as the nuclear family with a working father, the stay-at-home mother, and obedient children.

Many became hippies and lived loose lifestyles while doing drugs. Hippies were known for wanting peace, their tie-dye clothes, and their anti-establishment views. Rock and roll also became popular, and Elvis Presley and the Beatles were extremely popular musicians. Ultimately, China's Cultural Revolution was more violent, but America's "revolution" is still a pervasive part of its current society.

Exciting Entry

On this day in 1909, U Thant was born. From Burma, he served in Burma's government for several years before representing them in the UN. He served as the UN's secretary-general from 1961 to 1971.

Prominent Passing

On this day in 1973, Lyndon B. Johnson died. President following President Kennedy's assassination, Johnson expanded US involvement in Vietnam and signed the Civil Rights Act of 1964 into law.

CAMP DAVID PEACE ACCORDS

Exciting Entry

On this day in 1918, Gertrude Elion was born. She helped develop drugs to treat leukemia and several other diseases. She and two other people earned the Nobel Peace Prize in Physiology or Medicine in 1988.

Prominent Passing

On this day in 1989, Salvador Dalí died. A Surrealist artist, Dalí's unique style brought him much acclaim. His most iconic piece was *The Persistence of Memory,* which is full of wilted, melted watches.

In 1979, the historic Israel-Egypt peace agreement was signed. A few months earlier, President Jimmy Carter had helped to negotiate the Camp David Accords. This was the first peace treaty between Israel and any of its Arab neighbors since Israel had officially become a nation in 1948.

For their work on the treaty, Israeli Prime Minister Menachem Begin and Egyptian President Anwar el-Sadat received the Nobel Prize for Peace. The location of the accords that Carter helped to negotiate was Camp David, a sort of "presidential getaway." Camp David was a favorite of many presidents.

Franklin Delano Roosevelt was the first president to use Camp David. The WPA built the camp, then called Hi-Catoctin, as a getaway for federal employees. The campground was then renamed Shangri-La. Dwight Eisenhower renamed the camp after his grandson, David Eisenhower. Although he had originally planned to shut down the camp, describing it as a "luxury," he changed his mind after visiting it.

The exact location of the Camp is kept hidden from the public for safety reasons, and much of the staff is made up of members from the Navy and Marines. Ronald Reagan enjoyed watching movies at Camp David with his friends and family, watching 344 movies in total. While many presidents use the retreat to relax, the camp has also had its fair share of use for political reasons.

THREE MILE ISLAND ACCIDENT

On March 28, 1979, the worst accident in the United States' nuclear power industry occurred. In the early morning hours at Three Mile Island, a pressure valve failed, which caused the core to dangerously overheat.

The Three Mile Island Nuclear Generating Station, located in Dauphin County, Pennsylvania, was built during the late 1960s and 1970s and was able to provide electricity for the region by the end of the 1970s. On March 28, 1979, the Unit 2 reactor experienced a partial meltdown. The plant's staff took steps to fix the problem; however, it only made the situation worse.

Pennsylvania Governor Dick Thornburgh did not want to cause a mass panic by ordering an evacuation, but he considered the option. Two days later, the discovery of a highly flammable bubble of hydrogen gas revealed that radiation had leaked into the atmosphere. Upon this discovery, Governor Thornburgh advised a few people to evacuate but more than 100,000 people fled the area.

Remarkable Remark

"I was getting about one-third the radiation in the control room that I would have been getting if I was in an airplane flying from Washington to Los Angeles at 35,000-foot altitude."

—*Jimmy Carter*

Exciting Entry

On this day in 1921, Bernard James Dwyer was born. A New Jersey politician, Dwyer served six terms in the House of Representatives and was known for his behind-the-scenes work to pass legislation.

Prominent Passing

On this day in 1965, Winston Churchill died. Great Britain's prime minister during WWII, Churchill also served again from 1951 to 1955. He was one of the first world leaders to recognize the evils of communism.

President Jimmy Carter, a trained nuclear engineer, visited the plant to inspect it and to also give a reassuring presence to the local residents. Little harm came to the area surrounding Three Mile Island, but the cleanup effort cost roughly a billion dollars and took fourteen years to complete.

Jan 25

1980 OLYMPICS BAN

Remarkable Remark
"The Soviets want very much to have athletes come to Moscow. The Olympic boycott has hurt them very badly in world opinion and also within their own country."
—*Jimmy Carter*

Exciting Entry
On this day in 1933, Corazon Aquino was born. She was president of the Philippines from 1986 to 1992 and helped create a new constitution following the removal of Filipino dictator Ferdinand Marcos.

Prominent Passing
On this day in 2017, Mary Tyler Moore died. A popular actress throughout the Cold War, Moore starred in fan-favorite series like *The Dick Van Dyke Show* and *The Mary Tyler Moore Show*.

President Trump's calling on the NFL to suspend players who would not stand for the national anthem was not the first time in American history in which politics were mingled with sports.

In 1980, President Jimmy Carter informed the US Olympic team that because of the Soviet invasion of Afghanistan, the United States would be boycotting that year's Olympic Games, which were being held in Moscow. This marked the first (and currently only) time in which the United States boycotted the Olympics.

Many of the athletes were conflicted about whether or not to support the president's wishes or perform in many of their career's defining moments. Although they felt like the president was politicizing the international competitions, most of the athletes reluctantly supported Carter. Carter also imposed other economic sanctions on the Soviet Union and convinced several other nations to join the boycott.

Despite the move, there is no visible evidence of the boycott having any effect on the Soviet foreign policy. The Soviet military did not begin withdrawing from Afghanistan for almost a decade; however, it can be argued that the prestige of the games played in Moscow was diminished by the absence of one of the world superpowers. In retaliation to the United States boycott of the 1980 Moscow Olympics, the Soviet Union boycotted the 1984 Los Angeles Olympics.

 **DON'T DRINK THE KOOL-AID**

"Drink the Kool-Aid" is an American idiom which means to blindly follow a person or group. But many do not know where this idiom originated.

On November 18, 1978, in Jonestown, Guyana, more than nine hundred people died from cyanide poisoning. The leader, Jim Jones, had founded several "churches" throughout California between the 1950s and the 1970s to create a utopia. Members were regularly humiliated, beaten, and blackmailed, and many were coerced or brainwashed into signing over their possessions—including their homes—to the church. As the media began to investigate him, Jim Jones fled to a compound that he had built in Guyana.

In Guyana, Jones found more autonomy than he had in California. However, when a United States Congressman, Leo Ryan, visited Jones's compound, members who were being held against their will tried to escape. Members who still believed in Jones launched an attack on Congressman Ryan and his party, leading to Ryan's death.

Remarkable Remark

"I obviously don't think that the Jonestown cult was typical in any way of America. I think these were people who became obsessed with a particular leader's philosophy."
—Jimmy Carter

Exciting Entry

On this day in 1918, Nicolae Ceausescu was born. He was the communist leader of Romania for over two decades. Ceausescu openly opposed the Soviet Union's attempted control over Communist Romania.

Prominent Passing

On this day in 1979, Nelson Rockefeller died. He became Ford's vice president following President Nixon's resignation and was the the second vice president to not have been elected by the Electoral College.

Upon hearing the news, Jim Jones ordered everyone in and around the compound to commit suicide, using a fruit drink laced with cyanide. Jones himself was later found dead with a gunshot wound. While the drink mix used was Flavor Aid, many began substituting Flavor Aid for Kool-Aid. So, whatever you do, don't "drink the Kool-Aid."

Jan **27**

RONALD REAGAN'S JOKE

During the Cold War, presidents had to be extremely careful when speaking, as the slightest slipup could have disastrous consequences. In 1984, President Ronald Reagan made a joke that led to international embarrassment.

As he was preparing for his weekly radio broadcast, one of the workers asked him to do a sound check. Reagan obliged, declaring that he had just ordered the bombing and destruction of Russia. While this was not actually broadcast, his words were soon leaked and became an embarrassment to the Reagan administration and the United States as a whole.

Foreign media considered Reagan to be irresponsible and declared that his comments were not of the proper level of seriousness for a president of the United States. Reagan's joke provided additional ammunition for commentators at home and abroad who believed that the anticommunist crusader was reckless and intent on provoking a conflict with the Soviet Union. The Soviet Union as a whole attacked the president for his remarks.

Fortunately, Reagan's comment had no effect on his relationship with the Soviet leader Mikhail Gorbachev, as they would go on to later sign the Intermediate-Range Nuclear Forces Treaty in 1987, eliminating certain nuclear weapons. While it was not Reagan's first time making an embarrassing quip, the response to this one probably got his attention.

ARTHUR WALKER

In 1985, Arthur Walker, a Soviet spy from one of the most significant Cold War spy rings, was found guilty of espionage.

Arthur Walker worked as a defense contractor. He was found guilty of espionage for passing top-secret military documents to his brother John, who then passed the documents to Soviet agents. Both brothers were retired Navy veterans.

The investigation of the Walker brothers began after John's wife informed the FBI of her husband's involvement in the spy ring. She reported him to the government because she was angry because of their divorce.

Arthur Walker was sentenced to life in prison, while his brother John received two life sentences, putting an end to what the US government claimed was one of the most destructive spy rings during the Cold War. John was the one who got Arthur initially involved with the Soviets; however, he got off with the lighter sentence.

Despite the government's claim, Arthur insisted until his death in 2014 that his actions had no real influence on the security of the US military, as the papers that he stole were the lowest level of classification. During the trial, it was difficult to determine how involved Arthur wanted to be in espionage, and many concluded he was more of a pawn. Walker shocked America as many did not think that a retired American veteran would betray his country.

Remarkable Remark

"The Soviets gained access to weapons and sensor data, naval tactics, terrorist threats, surface, submarine and airborne training, readiness and tactics."
— Secretary of Defense Caspar Weinberger

Exciting Entry

On this day in 1905, Luther George Simjian was born. Simjian helped develop the automatic teller machine (ATM) and held another two hundred patents, including several inventions used by the military.

Prominent Passing

On this day in 1986, the *Challenger* broke apart. The astronauts who died were Ellison Onizuka, Christa McAuliffe, Gregory Jarvis, Judith Resnick, Michael Smith, Francis Scobee, and Ronald McNair.

TIANANMEN SQUARE

Remarkable Remark

"After the tragedy of Tiananmen, the United States was the first nation to condemn the use of violence against the peacefully demonstrating people of Beijing."
—*George H. W. Bush*

Exciting Entry

On this day in 1945, Donna Caponi was born. A prominent female golfer throughout the Cold War, Caponi played her way to 24 wins. She was inducted into the World Golf Hall of Fame in 2001.

Prominent Passing

On this day in 1963, Robert Frost died. One of the US' greatest poets, his voluminous writings won him numerous awards. In the late 1950s, he was the poetry consultant for the Library of Congress.

Many times, people become so used to freedom that they focus on what they do not have instead of what they do. But we cannot forget those that would love to be in our situation.

In 1989, roughly one million Chinese college students were marching through the streets of Beijing, protesting with the hopes of receiving basic political rights. They were encouraged by the fact that the Chinese government had recently granted a few economic freedoms.

Drawing these people together was Hu Yaobang's death, a former Communist Party leader. Hu had worked to move China toward a more open political system and had become a symbol of democratic reform.

General Secretary of the Chinese Communist Party Zhao Ziyang appeared at the rally and pleaded for an end to the demonstrations. Zhao, who wanted China to introduce far-reaching political reforms, could not get the demonstrators to listen.

Eventually, the Chinese government decided that enough was enough and sent soldiers and tanks to end the protests. There are no confirmed numbers as to how many died, but most estimate numbers in the thousands. China to this day refuses to acknowledge these events that occurred in Tiananmen Square in 1989; however, the event is remembered elsewhere around the globe.

 **REAGAN AT THE MOVIES**

Ronald Reagan greatly enjoyed watching movies as president. He would go up to Camp David, many times with his wife and some friends, and would watch movies, new and old. As a former Hollywood star, it was seemingly in his blood to watch movies.

The movies that Reagan would watch affected his policies as president. When he watched *WarGames* (sic), he was terrified by the notion that someone could hack into the US computers and begin a nuclear war. He brought up such a possibility a few days later in a meeting with the Joint Chiefs of Staff. The response that he eventually received was that the problem was even worse. A fictional film led to the upgrading of computer security in the government.

Reagan's idea for the Strategic Defense Initiative was derisively called "Star Wars" by its critics. It called for a laser missile shield to protect the United States from the "Evil Empire" that was the Soviet Union. While Reagan had always been interested in this type of technology, with the film *Star Wars* released just a few years prior to Reagan's presidency, the defense inititive was named after the movie. Its plot revolved around an evil Empire which attempted to use a laser weapon to rule the universe. Funding was hard to obtain as the Strategic Defense Initiative was too advanced to be technologically feasible during the 1980s. Regardless, movies and Reagan's policies often seemed to be intertwined during his time in office.

Remarkable Remark
"The Strategic Defense Initiative has been labeled "Star Wars," but it isn't about war; it's about peace…. It isn't about fear; it's about hope."
—*Ronald Reagan*

Exciting Entry
On this day in 1925, Douglas Engelbart was born. A generally unknown inventor, Engelbart's most important invention is now used by millions of people every day. In 1964, he invented the computer mouse.

Prominent Passing
On this day in 1991, John Bardeen died. A physicist, Bardeen co-won the Nobel Prize in 1956 for his work with transistors, and he co-won again in 1972 for his work with the theory of superconductivity.

Jan **31**

FALL OF THE BERLIN WALL

Remarkable Remark

"If you [Gorbachev] seek peace, if you seek prosperity...if you seek liberalization: Come here to this gate! Mr. Gorbachev, open this gate! Mr. Gorbachev, tear down this wall!"

—*Ronald Reagan*

Exciting Entry

On this day in 1919, Jack (Jackie) Robinson was born. Robinson is remembered for breaking the color barrier in baseball. In 1997, his number, 42, was retired by every MLB team in his honor.

Prominent Passing

On this day in 2015, Richard von Weizsäcker died. Weizsäcker served as the president of West Germany from 1984 to 1990 and was the first president of a unified Germany, as the Cold War came to an end.

Following WWII, Germany was eventually split into Communist East Germany and capitalist West Germany. However, Berlin, which was in East Germany, was also split into communist East and capitalistic West Berlin.

In an effort to keep the tens of thousands of East Berliners from crossing the border into freedom, the Communist government began building a wall on August 13, 1961. The wall, which took about two weeks to build, was constructed of concrete and barbed wire.

Following its completion, President Kennedy visited Berlin and gave his famous speech near the iconic Brandenburg Gate. The wall did help to diffuse the current political and military situation in the area; however, it left many oppressed in East Berlin.

In 1987, President Ronald Reagan visited the Berlin Wall and made his famous speech when he told Soviet Premier Mikhail Gorbachev to get rid of the Berlin Wall. Interestingly enough, Gorbachev was not too worried about Reagan's declaration. In 1989, the Berlin Wall came down, reuniting the East and West Berliners once again. People on both sides used hammers to chip away at the wall, and later bulldozers destroyed the Berlin Wall. The fall of the Berlin Wall essentially ended the Cold War, and the global age began.

February

BLACK HISTORY MONTH

In 1963, over 250,000 people descended upon Washington D.C. for their March on Washington. The culmination of the event was Martin Luther King Jr.'s "I Have A Dream" speech. King and other civil rights leaders continued the efforts of their ancestors for equality for all Americans. Black Americans' achievements have been overlooked, yet they are all a vital part of American history.

Since history has been recorded, blacks have had an important part in the world. Several important, powerful black people ruled in Africa and Asia for over hundreds of years, and it was not until after the European Dark Ages that their accomplishments began to be ignored. For hundreds of years, millions of Africans were captured by opposing African tribes, sold as slaves to the Europeans, and forced to work as slaves across the world. Because of slavery, many accomplishments, especially in the United States, were passed over. It is important to recognize that Black Americans have made numerous advancements for the United States of America and the black American community, but it is equally important to recognize that first and foremost, we are all Americans.

SLAVE TURNED POET

Remarkable Remark

"Twas mercy brought me from my *Pagan* land,

Taught my benighted soul to understand

That there's a God, that there's a *Saviour* to."
—*On Being Brought from AFRICA to AMERICA*

Exciting Entry

On this day in 1902, Langston Hughes was born. Hughes is best known for his writing during the Harlem Renaissance on racial justice. Recent research suggests he was actually born in 1901.

Prominent Passing

On this day in 1959, Madame Sul-Te-Wan died. In her multi-decade career, she acted alongside Lucille Ball, Rock Hudson, Fred Mac-Murray, Gloria Swanson, Buster Keaton, and many other famous actors.

Phyllis Wheatley was the first African American to publish a book and to make a living from her writings. It was her writing that created the foundation for African American literature.

It is believed that Phyllis was taken from West Africa around 1753. She got her name from the ship that brought her to America and took her master's last name of Wheatley following her baptism. Although she did not speak English when she first arrived, she could read English, Greek, and Latin before she died around the age of thirty-one.

Her first poem was written when she was about thirteen, and she published a book soon after. Since Boston publishers refused to publish a book written by a slave, Phyllis had her book published in London. Her best-known poem, "On Being Brought from AFRICA to AMERICA," brought her prominence throughout the colonies. However, she ultimately died in poverty after her husband left her.

Her life was an anomaly as she learned more than many free men in the colonies would ever learn, let alone slaves. She was given an invitation to visit George Washington to read a poem in his honor, and Benjamin Franklin praised her work. She believed that the institution of slavery held the colonies back from fully achieving their goal of freedom. In 2003, a statue in her honor was placed in Boston, and her life inspired many Americans of her day.

FOUNDING OF THE AME CHURCH

Richard Allen was born a slave and became a Methodist at seventeen. At the age of twenty-two, he began preaching, and four years later he bought his freedom. Allen was one of America's first religious and civil rights leaders.

He moved to Philadelphia and joined St. George's Methodist Church where he occasionally preached and led a Bible study for black people. However, the Methodist church restricted the number who could attend, and several incidents of racism caused Allen to leave the church.

He finally decided to start his own church, which originally met in a converted blacksmith shop. In 1816, the African Methodist Episcopal (AME) Church was founded and Richard Allen became the church's first bishop.

Allen was also an active opponent against the American Colonization Society. He organized a group to help the poor and widowed and provided aid during the Philadelphia yellow fever epidemic in 1793. During the epidemic, Allen and his supporters took care of the sick and buried the dead.

Remarkable Remark
"I was confident that…no religious sect…would suit the capacity of the colored people as well as the Methodist; for the plain and simple gospel suits best for any people."
—*Richard Allen*

Exciting Entry
On this day in 1914, William Artis was born. He was a famous master sculptor and taught at several schools around the country. Artis's works have been exhibited in collections around the United States.

Prominent Passing
On this day in 1990, Joel Fluellen died. As an actor, he worked to end black stereotypes in Hollywood. He appeared on *Alfred Hitchcock Presents*, *The Dick Van Dyke Show*, and dozens of other shows.

He wrote pamphlets against slavery and even used his church building as a stop in the Underground Railroad. Today, the denomination he founded has over six thousand churches and over two million members. Richard Allen's legacy for equality and freedom of worship continues to this day.

DEFEATING RACISM IN THE OREGON COUNTRY

Remarkable Remark

"Not many men of color left a slave state so well to do, and so generally respected; but it was not in the nature of things that he should be permitted to forget his color."

—*Description of Bush*

Exciting Entry

On this day in 1879, Charles Follis was born. He played football and was the first African American to be paid as a professional football player. He played for Ohio's Shelby Blues from 1902 to 1906.

Prominent Passing

On this day in 1999, Gwen Guthrie died. She was a songwriter and singer and sang lead and backing vocalist for numerous songs. She was one of the first recording artists to raise money to fight AIDS.

George Washington Bush was the child of a free African American servant and an Irish maiden. Bush fought alongside General Andrew Jackson during the War of 1812. After the war, he became a trapper, first independently and later for the Hudson Bay Company. He eventually moved to Missouri and began a highly successful farm.

Sadly, racism was strong in the slave state of Missouri in the early 1800s. To escape oppression, Bush, his wife, his five sons, and a party of thirty-two other settlers headed out west. Many of these settlers were poor, and Bush and his partner Michael Simmons were known for helping their fellow travelers financially.

When the party arrived in the Oregon Territory, they made a sad discovery: the Oregon Provisional Government had set up Black Exclusion Laws. Blacks found in Oregon were subject to twenty to thirty-nine lashes every six months. Not desiring this treatment, Bush and his party went north of the Columbia River and established the city of Tumwater, the first American settlement in this territory, later known as Washington. Territorial laws like the Black Exclusion Laws were going to expand into where Bush had settled; however, the citizens of Tumwater and the surrounding areas petitioned to Congress. Their plea was heard, and the Bush family continued to prosper in Tumwater.

THE LIFE OF SOJOURNER TRUTH

Sojourner Truth, born Isabelle Baumfree, was an African American abolitionist and women's rights activist. She was originally a slave in New York, serving multiple masters.

She gained her freedom after the state enacted an emancipation law. However, several of her children were retained as property. Sojourner Truth escaped with her daughter but had to sue to get her son back. In 1828, she became the first African American to win such a case against a white man.

Following her and her family gaining freedom, she began working as a housekeeper for a few preachers. It was during this time that Baumfree changed her name to Sojourner Truth and felt it her religious obligation to speak against the evils of slavery.

Later on, Sojourner Truth became a vocal advocate of women's rights. In 1844, she joined the abolitionist Northampton Association of Education and Industry in Massachusetts, where she met Frederick Douglass and began fighting for equal rights. She is best remembered for her speech "Ain't I a Woman," which she delivered at the 1851 Ohio Women's Rights Convention in Akron. She would finish her life trying to secure land grants for freed slaves after the Civil War. She was listed by the Smithsonian Magazine in 2014 as one of the top one hundred most significant Americans.

Remarkable Remark

"I have heard the bible and have learned that Eve caused man to sin. Well if woman upset the world, do give her a chance to set it right side up again."
—"Ain't I A Woman" speech

Exciting Entry

On this day in 1913, Rosa Parks was born. She is best remembered as an activist who refused to leave her bus seat. Many consider her refusal to be what helped to spark the Civil Rights movement.

Prominent Passing

On this day in 1975, Louis Jordan died. During the 1940s and 1950s, he became a prominent saxophonist and singer. Jordan also helped develop both rhythm and blues (R&B) and rock and roll.

 *Feb* **5**

MARTIN ROBINSON DELANY

Remarkable Remark

"Delany hasn't persisted in public view primarily because he was not nearly as elegant...I believe Delany is second only to Frederick Douglass...as a black leader."

—*John Stauffer*

Exciting Entry

On this day in 1934, Hank Aaron was born. He played twenty-three seasons in the MLB and was one of baseball's most prominent players. He beat Babe Ruth's home run record in 1974 and held it for about thirty years.

Prominent Passing

On this day in 1990, Ann Gregory died. She was the first African American woman to play in a United States Golf Association championship. Gregory used her talent to try to defeat racism in sports.

Martin Robinson Delany was a free African American who spent much of his lifetime working to end slavery. Abolitionist, physician, and soldier were just a few of the titles that he could claim.

Born in Charles Town, Virginia, in 1812, Martin Delany was legally free from birth because of a Virginia law stating that children were born with the same status that their mother had. Delany eventually was accepted into Harvard Medical School as one of the first black men to attend, but he was soon forced to depart because of protests from the other students.

In 1859, Delany sailed to West Africa to see whether or not free African Americans would be able to relocate and live in a country outside of the United States. Because of local warfare, white opposition, and the American Civil War, nothing permanent came from his trip.

In 1863, Martin Delany began recruiting black men to join Abraham Lincoln and the Union Army in their war against the Confederacy. He was also the first black man to receive a regular army commission when he was made a major in 1865. It is estimated that black men made up about 10% of the Union Army. Following the Civil War, Delany worked in the Freedmen's Bureau and unsuccessfully ran for lieutenant governor of South Carolina as an independent Republican. Delany remained very active politically up until his death in 1885.

NAT TURNER REVOLT

On August 21, 1831, Nat Turner began his revolt against the slave owners in Virginia, killing the majority of the slave owners in the area.

Hoping to capture an armory and lead a massive uprising against slave owners, Nat Turner instead massacred about fifty-five people and led the state militia and federal troops on a two-month long manhunt. Turner's followers, about sixty in number, were soon captured, but Turner himself was not captured until October.

Dozens of slaves stood trial for their participation in the rebellion, with some released and dozens more convicted and sentenced to death. In addition, revenge-minded white mobs lynched blacks who played no part in the uprising.

Legislation was passed to limit the education that slaves could receive, and legislators rejected legislation for gradual emancipation as was in the North. Nat Turner was hanged for his role as leader of this group on November 11, 1831. While not the largest or bloodiest, Turner's revolt is perhaps the most famous slave revolt in US history. Turner confessed without remorse and remained resigned to his fate.

One often overlooked fact is that the mob riots killed hundreds of innocent black slaves simply because Turner scared the slaveowners so badly. What Turner had hoped to be for good only hurt the plight of slaves more leading up to the Civil War.

Remarkable Remark

"The judgment of the court is, that you be taken…[and] hung by the neck until you are dead! dead! dead! and may the Lord have mercy upon your soul."
—*The Commonwealth vs. Nat Turner*

Exciting Entry

On this day in 1898, Melvin Tolson was born. Tolson was a popular poet who wrote following the Harlem Renaissance. He wrote optimistically, looking for a better future for African Americans.

Prominent Passing

On this day in 1993, Arthur Ashe died. He was the first black winner of a major men's single championship. He opposed South African apartheid and was banned from playing in the country.

THE STRUGGLES OF FREDERICK DOUGLASS

Frederick Douglass struggled all his life. Douglass was born in 1818 and lived on a plantation in Maryland where he was educated against the laws of the state. He eventually escaped to New England where he gained his freedom.

While there, he was asked to describe his experiences as a slave to an anti-slavery group. His speech was so well received that he became a spokesperson for the Massachusetts Anti-Slavery Society.

Douglass decided to publish his memoirs and went on a speaking tour in Great Britain and Ireland to avoid capture from his former master. Through his speaking, Douglass continued to gain friends for the abolitionist cause.

When Frederick returned, he bought his freedom and took his last name from a poem soon thereafter. He ran an anti-slavery newspaper and split on several issues with vocal abolitionist William Lloyd Garrison. He was an adviser to President Lincoln and supported the Union throughout the Civil War. Following Reconstruction, Douglass served in several government positions. He was also the first black person to be nominated for the vice presidency, and although he declined the chance to run for office, he continued to play an important part in politics. His life left a lasting legacy for future Americans and showed others that regardless of color, anyone can make a difference in American society.

UNDERGROUND RAILROAD CONDUCTOR

Harriet Tubman, born Araminta Ross, was a conductor on the Underground Railroad and military leader. Escaping from her owners in Maryland, she became a free woman after reaching Pennsylvania in 1849.

Tubman, realizing the need to free other people including her family, made several more trips to free slaves and lead them along the Underground Railroad. While a few writers claimed that Tubman led around three hundred slaves to freedom, this account has been discredited as an embellishment. In reality, she saved about seventy slaves during her time as a conductor on the Underground Railroad.

Rescuing family and non-family members alike, Tubman eventually had southern slaveholders place a bounty on her head. She received the name Moses because she freed slaves and never lost a single one, even drugging smaller children to keep them from crying out on the journey to freedom.

During the Civil War, Harriet Tubman worked as a nurse, cook, and spy for the Union army. For her service, she eventually earned a pension, but only after applying for several decades. During the Civil War, she led an assault to free slaves and attack influential southern leaders' properties. She lost none and rescued over seven hundred slaves. Her life of accomplishments and hard work has helped her gain international achievement, with some seeking to add her to the twenty dollar bill.

Remarkable Remark

"I was the conductor of the Underground Railroad for eight years, and I can say what most conductors can't say—I never ran my train off the track and I never lost a passenger."
—Harriet Tubman

Exciting Entry

On this day in 1968, Gary Coleman was born. Coleman became famous as the star of the NBC sitcom Diff'rent Strokes. His catchphrase "Whatcha talkin bout, Willis?" is still popular to this day.

Prominent Passing

On this day in 1996, Mercer Ellington died. He was the son of musician Duke Ellington and took over his father's band after he died. He wrote a biography about his father and later moved to Denmark.

CIVIL WAR HERO

In 1839, African American slave Robert Smalls was born. A generally forgotten name in US history, he was well known in his lifetime for his brave deeds and leadership.

Smalls was living as a slave in Charleston, South Carolina, where he worked. When the Civil War broke out, he was hired out to work on a Confederate ship named *Planter*. On May 13, 1862, Robert Smalls and the other black workers onboard took over the ship and sailed it past several Confederate checkpoints and surrendered it to a Union naval squadron.

For Smalls's bravery in taking a southern ship from a southern port and through southern checkpoints, all while being a slave, he was allowed to pilot a ship during a battle for Fort Sumter. When his ship was sunk, he was given command of the now Union ship, *Planter*, and became the first African American to captain a vessel in US service.

Following the Civil War, Smalls returned to South Carolina and became a state legislator. He was elected to the US House of Representatives, where he served from 1875 to 1879 and 1882 to 1887. However, he was accused of taking a bribe while in the state senate and was sentenced three years in prison. Smalls was eventually pardoned as the case was politically motivated. He was one of the first black men to serve in Congress and helped pave the way for future minorities to serve in Congress.

GEORGE WASHINGTON BUCKNER

The life of George Washington Buckner is inspiring but it is often passed by in the pages of history. He was born a slave in the small town of Greensburg, Kentucky, in 1855 and gained his freedom in 1865 at the end of the Civil War.

Buckner attended a Freedmen's School for his basic education and eventually went to Indiana State Normal School (currently Indiana State University) to learn how to teach. He began to teach, but ultimately decided to go to Indiana Eclectic Medical College, where he obtained a degree in medicine.

Following Buckner's educational endeavors, he taught at several different schools, became a staunch Democrat, was a newspaper editor, and was a proud member of the Alexander Chapel African Methodist Episcopal (AME) Church. He also helped start the Cherry Street Black YMCA.

He was close friends with Democrat congressman John Boehne, and through connections in the Democratic Party, he was introduced to President Woodrow Wilson. Wilson soon appointed Bucker as the US minister to the nation of Liberia in 1913 and as the US Consul General in Monrovia, Liberia in 1914. Buckner was the first African American to be appointed as a foreign minister from the United States. He resigned the post because of illness in 1915 and went on to practice medicine. He became an advocate for civil rights until his death in 1943.

Remarkable Remark

"I was interested in [helping] the young people and anxious for their advancement but the suffering endured by my invalid mother… would not desert my consciousness."
—G. W. Buckner

Exciting Entry

On this day in 1927, Leontyne Price was born. Price was the first African American to gain international respect as an opera singer. She was awarded the Presidential Medal of Freedom in 1964.

Prominent Passing

On this day in 1992, Alex Haley died. His first major work as an author was an autobiography of Malcolm X. His book *Roots: The Saga of an American Family* was adapted as the television program, *Roots*.

 Feb 11

BLACK WALL STREET

In the early part of the twentieth century, Tulsa, Oklahoma's Greenwood black district was considered one of the richest black communities in America. However, in 1921, one of the worst atrocities in the United States occurred in this community.

In a section of the city called Black Wall Street, many men and women had found great wealth. Prosperous businesses, farmers, and oil tycoons had built the black community into one of the richest communities in the country, regardless of color. Money stayed in the community and continued to build a prosperous neighborhood.

Yet greed and jealousy by the surrounding community for the prosperous black neighborhood led to a level of violence few could imagine. Led by the KKK and local officials, mobs began to attack the prosperous Black Wall Street.

The mobs dropped bombs from the air and began burning and looting houses and businesses. In less than a day, hundreds of black citizens were killed and over six hundred businesses were destroyed. Surviving witnesses said that many white families stood on the outskirts of the community and watched as the destruction unfolded.

For decades, media and state officials covered up the riots, and news headlines and official documentation could not be found. It wasn't until 2001 that a report on the matter officially came out.

GEORGE WASHINGTON CARVER

George Washington Carver was born into slavery in 1864 (his exact birthday is unknown). He would later gain his freedom and enter into the field of botany at Iowa State. Shortly thereafter, he was recruited by Booker T. Washington to lead the agricultural department at the Tuskegee Institute.

After the decline of cotton in the South, agriculture was suffering from over-planting, and Carver sought to resolve this issue. His plan was to plant peanuts and soybeans to replenish the nitrogen in the soil. This would lead to his most famous accomplishment. Carver is thought to have created over 260 products from the peanut alone, ranging from milk, plastics, cosmetics, paints, and soap. His creativity eventually earned him the nickname "the Peanut Man."

However, Carver also found numerous other uses for seemingly useless plants, including some 118 sweet potato products, some 85 pecan products, and synthesized rubber made from soybeans. Carver called his laboratory "God's Little Workshop." He believed he needed to help the poor southerners, regardless of color, rebuild their farms.

After years of fame and hard work, Carver died after falling down the stairs in his home on January 5, 1943. He was seventy-eight. Carver did much to help African American equality in a divisive time.

Remarkable Remark

"He could have added fortune to fame but caring for neither he found happiness and honor in being helpful to the world."
—G.W. Carver's epitaph

Exciting Entry

On this day in 1949, Lenny Randle was born. An MLB player, he is best known for beating up his manager over a starting position and for physically blowing a baseball into foul territory over the third base line.

Prominent Passing

On this day in 1983, Eubie Blake died. He was a popular ragtime composer and pianist. His work in Vaudeville contributed greatly to the Harlem Renaissance and ultimately led to the Jazz Age in the 1920s.

W.E.B. DU BOIS

Exciting Entry

On this day in 1873, Emmett Scott was born. He was Booker Washington's secretary and the highest-ranking black member in the Wilson government, serving as special assistant to the secretary of war.

Prominent Passing

On this day in 1818, Absalom Jones died. Jones, his friend Richard Allen, and others founded the Free African Society and later separated from the Methodist church because of racial discrimination.

William Edward Burghardt Du Bois is a name less familiar in the US Civil Rights history than names such as Frederick Douglass, Booker T. Washington, Martin Luther King, Jr. However, that should not diminish the accomplishments of W. E. B. Du Bois.

Du Bois was a prominent black protestor and helped found the National Association for the Advancement of Colored People (NAACP) in 1909. He also edited the NAACP's magazine and wrote several important pieces in African American literature.

Perhaps one reason that his name is not as familiar to many is that his methods were more extreme than others such as Booker T. Washington. He believed that because of the pervasive racism of the day, change would only be brought by agitation and protests. This was in direct contrast to B. T. Washington's view that blacks should accept discrimination while working hard and ultimately gain the respect of white men.

W. E. B. Du Bois wrote several essays and letters opposing white superiority and promoting the growing women's rights movement. Du Bois later became a leader of the first Pan-African Conference in London and helped form four Pan-African Congresses from 1919 to 1927. W. E. B. Du Bois died on August 27, 1963—the day before Martin Luther King gave his "I Have a Dream" speech.

"THE KING OF RAGTIME"

Scott Joplin was one of the best-known African American composers and pianists. Joplin was born a few years after the end of the Civil War and spent his early childhood in Texas.

Joplin loved music from an early age and was trained by family friends. Joplin eventually traveled to the South on a tour during the 1880s as an itinerant musician. He toured parts of the country and even performed at the World's Columbian Exposition (World's Fair) of 1893 in Chicago.

Joplin continued to study piano, hoping to become a concert pianist and composer. His first works, which included ragtime pieces, helped him gain fame, and he moved to St. Louis to continue his career. However, after some success, he had a nervous breakdown and was institutionalized in 1916.

Joplin became famous for the ragtime style. His most famous pieces are "The Maple Leaf Rag" and "The Entertainer." His work with ragtime earned Joplin the title "The King of Ragtime." Joplin's death in 1917 is considered the end of the ragtime era, but his songs and style were revived in the 1970s because of its use in films. Scott Joplin remains one of America's best musicians and was inducted into the Songwriters Hall of Fame in 1970. Joplin was also posthumously awarded a special Bicentennial Pulitzer Prize in 1976 in honor of his contribution to American music.

Remarkable Remark

"Play slowly until you catch the swing, and never play ragtime fast at any time."
—From Scott Joplin's School of Ragtime

Exciting Entry

On this day in 1760, Richard Allen was born. He split from the Methodist church and founded the African Methodist Episcopal Church. He was also the African Methodist Episcopal Church's first bishop.

Prominent Passing

On this day in 1959, Baby Dodds died. He was a popular jazz percussionist and one of the first jazz drummers to be recorded. He recorded songs with Louis Armstrong and was a leading jazz musician.

 **JAMES WELDON JOHNSON**

James Weldon Johnson was an African American author, lawyer, diplomat, songwriter, and civil rights activist.

Johnson was born in Jacksonville, Florida, in 1871, and was educated by his mother, who was a schoolteacher. He went on to study at Atlanta University and Columbia University.

Soon after his university studies, Johnson took the Florida bar exam, becoming the first African American allowed into the Florida Bar Exam since Reconstruction had ended. Johnson later wrote the poem "Lift Every Voice and Sing," which he and his brother would eventually set to music.

In 1901, Johnson and his brother went to New York, where they wrote roughly two hundred songs for Broadway musicals. In 1906, he was appointed consul to Venezuela, and in 1909, he was appointed consul in Nicaragua until 1914.

Johnson would teach at Fisk University and write an autobiography following his time as consul. He also led the National Association for the Advancement of Colored People (NAACP) for several years. He fought against the disenfranchisement of African Americans in the southern states. In 1927, Johnson published one of his most well-known works, *God's Trombones*, which included the popular poems "The Creation" and "Go Down Death." James Weldon Johnson was influential in leading America toward true freedom for all.

A WORLD FAMOUS POET

Paul Laurence Dunbar was the first African American poet to achieve worldwide recognition and was known for his dialectic writing.

Some of Dunbar's most recognized poems are "We Wear the Mask," "Life's Tragedy," and "Ships that Pass in the Night." These poems, along with his works done in a southern dialect, helped to shape American literature. Dunbar attended Central High School in Dayton, Ohio, and was the only African American in his graduating class. Orville Wright was also in this class, but Orville did not graduate.

One of his first jobs was as an elevator operator. During the small amount of free time that this job afforded, he wrote poems and spoke at the Western Associations of Writers. During this time, he received the nickname "Elevator Poet Boy." Throughout his writing career that lasted only thirteen years, Dunbar wrote almost four hundred poems and several novels, lyrics, and short stories; and was also the first African American poet to meet the queen of England.

Remarkable Remark

"Yea, though I walk through the valley of the shadow of death."
—*Dunbar's final words recited from Psalm 23 as written in the KJV*

Exciting Entry

On this day in 1957, Levar Burton was born. He starred in the miniseries *Roots* and in several *Star Trek* movies. He is also a major advocate for getting children interested in reading at a young age.

Prominent Passing

On this day in 1996, Brownie McGhee died. He was a prominent blues singer and musician and performed alongside blues performer Sonny Terry. In 1997, McGhee was inducted into the Blues Hall of Fame.

For just a short time, Dunbar worked as a clerk for the Library of Congress; during this time, Dunbar published several works that were well received. However, he had to leave this post because of a battle with tuberculosis, which eventually took his life. He was reading Psalm 23 to his mother as he breathed his last breaths.

 **Feb 17**

THE LEGACY OF BLIND WILLIE JOHNSON

Exciting Entry
On this day in 1963, Michael Jordan was born. He is often viewed as basketball's best player and led the Chicago Bulls to six championships. He was awarded the Presidential Medal of Freedom in 2016.

Prominent Passing
On this day in 1982, Thelonious Monk died. He was a talented musician who helped usher in modern jazz. He posthumously was awarded a Pulitzer Prize in 2006 for his contribution to the realm of music.

Blind Willie Johnson was born near Temple, Texas, in 1897. When he was only five years old, he built a small guitar out of a cigar box and proclaimed that he would become a preacher.

When he was seven years old, Johnson's life changed forever. During a dispute, his stepmother accidentally threw lye water into his eyes, permanently blinding him. With few options left besides guitar playing and preaching, he continued to develop these abilities, often traveling and preaching and playing to those who would listen.

Though many blues artists at the time used a bottleneck guitar slide, he used the back of a pocketknife! In 1927, Columbia Records had him record a session, and he quickly became their bestselling colored artist, though he received minimal payment. In 1947, his home in Beaumont, Texas, burned to the ground. With nowhere to go, he continued to sleep in the ashes of his home and soon contracted pneumonia and died a few weeks later.

Thankfully, his legacy did not stop there. During the '60s, his music again gained popularity during what is known as the "Blues Revival." In 1977 when NASA launched the *Voyager* spacecraft, they included a record in case the spacecraft was ever found by future humans or another life form. On the record were works by Mozart, Beethoven, and Blind Willie Johnson's song "Dark Was the Night, Cold was the Ground."

BENJAMIN O. DAVIS JR.

Benjamin O. Davis Jr. was a brave American soldier and hero. He was the first African American Air Force general, and he helped integrate black soldiers into the military.

Born in 1912, Benjamin Davis Jr. persevered through hardships to become an American hero. He attended West Point and later taught at Tuskegee. He was also one of only five African Americans to complete the flight training course there. In 1942, he became commander of the 99th Pursuit Squadron, also known as the Tuskegee Airmen.

After WWII, President Truman began to integrate black soldiers into the military and assigned Davis to help draft the Air Force integration plan. In 1949, he became the first African American to attend the Air War College and went on to command dozens of places around the globe. In 1960, he was promoted to Brigadier General and then to Major General in 1962. Davis retired from his military career in 1970 after more than thirty years of service. In 1998, President Clinton decorated him with the four-star insignia, giving Davis the rank of General, US Air Force (retired).

Remarkable Remark
"General Davis…[has proven] that from diversity we can build an even stronger unity and that in diversity we can find the strength to prevail and advance."
—*President Clinton*

Exciting Entry
On this day in 1931, Toni Morrison was born. She was a prolific author whose awards included the Pulitzer Prize, Nobel Peace Prize, Presidential Medal of Freedom, and the Coretta Scott King Award.

Prominent Passing
On this day in 2013, Damon Harris died. He was a popular singer known for his falsetto singing. He was diagnosed with cancer and created a foundation to raise cancer awareness.

After military service, he commanded the Federal Sky Marshall Program and later worked as the Assistant Secretary of Transportation, Environment, Safety, and Consumer Affairs. His life represented what defeating stereotypes and racism can accomplish. Benjamin O. Davis Jr. was a true American who proved that anyone can be a hero.

THE KING OF "KRAZY KAT"

Today, few recognize the name George Herriman. However, Herriman published one of the best cartoon strips in the United States and was considered a leader in his field.

George Herriman was a New Orleans-born cartoonist whose most famous work was his cartoon strip entitled "Krazy Kat," a comic strip that was published in William Randolph Hearst's string of newspapers. The series ran for more than thirty years. Herriman also wrote several other comic strips; however, none were as famous or loved as "Krazy Kat."

The comic portrays the humorous relationships between Krazy Kat and Ignatz Mouse. While Krazy Kat liked Ignatz Mouse, Ignatz would have nothing to do with Krazy Kat and constantly would throw bricks at him. The other main cartoon character was the police officer, Offissa Pupp. Ignatz would throw bricks at Krazy Kat, who mistook the injurious projectiles as acts of affection, and Offissa Pupp would try to guard Krazy from the attacks by putting Ignatz in jail.

As the comic strip gained more and more popularity, Herriman moved to Hollywood to continue his drawings. Herriman's artistic genius inspired several other cartoonists including Charles Schultz (Peanuts) and Dr. Seuss. Surprisingly, Herriman used his avenue of cartoon drawing to promote new opportunities for black Americans and to inspire the next generation of cartoonists.

DR. SELMA BURKE

Dr. Selma Burke is a name few know, yet many have seen her work. Dr. Selma Burke was a descendant of slaves, who by some reports were owned on one side by Stonewall Jackson and on the other by Harriet Beecher Stowe. Selma's mother sought to get her daughter a good education, and Selma went on to get her doctorate.

Selma was well known for her artwork and worked mainly as a sculptor. During WWII, she drove a truck at a naval yard and continued to serve her country in any way she could. She earned countless awards and was admired for her work. Yet, for all her many achievements, few know her most famous work.

Selma entered a contest to create a profile portrait of President Franklin Roosevelt, and she was granted a meeting with him to be able to get a realistic profile for her artwork. Many historians today believe that because of limited time, John Sinnock based his dime on Selma's bronze plaque of FDR. Sinnock added his initials to the dime and received most of the recognition for it. While Sinnock and the United States Mint have stated that his work is original, the Smithsonian and the National Archives have recently been given credit to Selma Burke.

Today, more people are recognizing Selma Burke as the genius behind the dime. Her original work of FDR can be found in the Recorder of Deeds Building in Washington, D.C. still today.

Remarkable Remark

"This has happened to so many black people. I have never stopped fighting this man [Sinnock] and have never had anyone who cared enough to give me the credit."
—Selma Burke

Exciting Entry

On this day in 1927, Sidney Poitier was born. He was a black movie star who broke the color barrier in the movie industry, becoming the first black American to win an Academy Award for Best Actor.

Prominent Passing

On this day in 1895, Frederick Douglass died. Douglass, a leading abolitionist, was one of the best-known men in the nineteenth century. Douglass was also the most photographed man in the nineteenth century.

A RENOWNED AVIATRIX

Bessie Coleman was a young lady undaunted by the discrimination of her time and willing to fight for the things she enjoyed doing. Because of this determination, Coleman was the first female African American pilot in the United States.

Coleman had a love for learning at a young age and did very well at mathematics. She briefly went to college in Oklahoma before working in Chicago. It was in Chicago that she first became interested in the new field of aviation. However, she was unable to receive her pilot's license in the United States because of racial prejudice.

In turn, Coleman took an extraordinary step. She taught herself French and traveled to France, where she trained at the Caudron Brothers School of Aviation in France, with black philanthropists paying for her tuition. She continued her training in aviation by practicing parachuting and stunt flying.

She later returned to the States and pursued a successful career in stunt flying. She refused to fly before segregated crowds and would travel the country attempting to garner interest in flying in the black American community. Coleman even wanted to start a flying school. Unfortunately, Coleman lost her life in a flying accident when she was around thirty-four years old and never started the school. Bessie Coleman is a great example of what one can accomplish when convinced to follow one's dream.

Feb **22**

MARTIN LUTHER KING JR.'S DEATH

On April 4, Americans across the country honor the life of Martin Luther King Jr., as April 4th is the anniversary of his assassination. Have you ever wondered why he was standing on the balcony when he was assassinated?

Martin Luther King Jr. was a peaceful reformer who actively fought for civil rights by staging dozens of peaceful protests and giving many speeches.

However, what most people don't know is that he was a chain smoker, often smoking multiple packs a day. King kept this habit from most of his family, children, and media as he didn't want his children to follow his example. King's wife, Coretta, hated the habit and often checked his pockets when he got home to see if he was carrying any cigarettes.

King's solution was to have his driver hold his cigarettes so his wife wouldn't find them. The reason that King was on the balcony when he got shot was because he was smoking, and his friend removed the pack off his body before the police and media arrived. Very few photos exist showing King smoking; however, multiple close sources have verified the fact, and the photos that do exist of him smoking clearly show him smoking.

Martin Luther King Jr. made great advancements during the Civil Rights era. He is the reason many civil rights laws are in place. He was a great reformer and great man to those around him.

Remarkable Remark

"Injustice anywhere is a threat to justice every-where. We are caught in an inescapable network of mutuality, tied in a single garment of destiny. What-ever affects one directly, affects all indirectly."

—MLK Jr.

Exciting Entry

On this day in 1950, Julius Erving was born. Erving was a sensational basketball player, scoring over thirty thousand points in his career. He led his team, the Philadelphia 76ers, to a championship in 1983.

Prominent Passing

On this day in 1911, Frances Harper died. She was a writer and social reformer who advocated for abolition, women's suffrage, temperance, and helped start the National Association of Colored Women.

TRUMPETER LOUIS ARMSTRONG

Exciting Entry

On this day in 1868, W. E. B. Du Bois was born. He was a prominent protest leader in the early twentieth century and opposed Booker T. Washington's ideals for peacfully gaining black equality in American society.

Prominent Passing

On this day in 1915, Robert Smalls died. He was a slave who, during the Civil War, captured and surrendered a Confederate ship to the Union. He gained national prominence and served in Congress.

Louis Armstrong brought solo trumpet performances to the mainstream and was one of the first black musicians to be loved by people of all color. His hit songs included "Hello Dolly" and "What a Wonderful World."

Armstrong was born in an area of New Orleans called "The Battlefield" by locals. His early home life was hard, but he found a second home in the house of a Lithuanian Jewish family that helped him purchase his first cornet. Out of tribute to them, he occasionally wore a Star of David pendant.

Armstrong did not receive any musical lessons until he was eleven years old. These lessons were in the Colored Waif's Home for Boys, a juvenile detention center where he stayed eighteen months for firing a pistol.

Armstrong served the United States during the Cold War as a music ambassador. The United States sent many jazz musicians on goodwill tours around the world during the 1950s and 1960s. His tours were mainly in Africa, and he even stopped a war in the Congo when both sides signed a one day truce to come and hear him play.

One of Armstrong's most beloved songs is "What a Wonderful World." He recorded it in 1967, four years before his death, and it was considered a flop in the United States because of poor promotion. Twenty years later, it appeared in Robin Williams's movie *Good Morning, Vietnam*, which caused the song to enter the charts and become a worldwide favorite.

SUPREME COURT JUSTICE MARSHALL

In 1908, Thurgood Marshall was born. He was the first African American to serve on the Supreme Court.

Marshall went through law school and was taught that the law was a good avenue for social change. As a lawyer, he won several prominent cases and was soon the chief lawyer for the National Association for the Advancement of Colored People (NAACP).

He quickly made a name for himself throughout the 1940s and 1950s, winning nearly all the cases he argued before the US Supreme Court. Among his numerous prominent cases was *Brown v. Board of Education of Topeka*. In 1961, President John F. Kennedy nominated him to the US Court of Appeals. President Lyndon B. Johnson nominated him for the Supreme Court. In 1967, Marshall was confirmed.

All Supreme Court justices must take two oaths: Constitutional and Judicial. The constitutional oath was administered by Justice Hugo Black. Ironically, Hugo Black was once a member of the Ku Klux Klan during the height of its popularity. He was only a member for about two years and claimed to only be a member because other lawyers were joining to advance their careers and to make the group less radical. Both Black and Marshall became good friends and helped shape America as we know it today. Both fought for civil rights and helped protect the liberties that we enjoy today.

Remarkable Remark
"[Although not currently happening, a] child born to a black mother... has exactly the same rights as a white baby born to the wealthiest person in the United States."
—*Thurgood Marshall*

Exciting Entry
On this day in 1977, Floyd Mayweather Jr. was born. He was a prominent boxer known for his unique boxing style. He fought several big-name opponents and is currently retired from boxing with a 50-0 record.

Prominent Passing
On this day in 2007, Lamar Lundy died. He was a defensive end for the LA Rams and played thirteen seasons with the Rams. He was a member of the Ram's defensive line nicknamed the Fearsome Foursome.

 **JESSE OWENS: OLYMPIC ATHLETE**

Remarkable Remark

"People said it was de-grading for an Olympic champion to run against a horse, but what was I supposed to do? I had four gold medals, but you can't eat four gold medals."

—Jesse Owens

Exciting Entry

On this day in 1951, Donald Quarrie was born. Quarrie was an Olympic athlete from Jamaica who won one bronze medal, two silver medals, and one gold medal over three Olympic games as a sprinter.

Prominent Passing

On this day in 1975, Elijah Muhammad died. He was a religious leader of the Black Muslims, better known as the Nation of Islam. He was jailed for violating the Selective Service Act during WWII.

James Cleveland Owens, better known as "Jesse" Owens, was an African American track and field athlete who competed during the Berlin Olympics in 1936.

He succeeded in claiming the gold in several Olympic categories: 100-meter, 200-meter, long jump, and 4x100 relay. Recognized as the most accomplished athlete at the 1936 games, Owens shattered the German idea of the perfect Aryan race by beating his competition. His athleticism also helped the African American cause in the United States as well.

Unfortunately, Owens was not invited to the White House because of the racial barrier that existed at the time. He even felt like President Franklin Roosevelt shunned him. In contrast, Hitler did honor Jesse Owens's accomplishments. Soon after the Olympics, Owens had a hard time finding work. One way he earned money was by racing horses. From stadium races to half-time shows, Owens raced to earn money. Once a symbol of freedom and American might, he was soon a sideshow at other events.

Owens later was given the Presidential Medal of Freedom in 1976 and was posthumously awarded the Congressional Gold Medal in 1990. Owens remains as one of the most accomplished and influential American athletes of all time.

EARLY ATTEMPTS TO END SLAVERY

Perhaps no other issue has been as divisive in American history then slavery. However, from the beginning, men saw the evils of slavery and tried to do their part to end it.

The first attempt was in 1688, when Quakers in Pennsylvania wrote a two-page condemnation of the slavery practice and sent it to the governing bodies of their Quaker church. Thomas Paine, writer of *Common Sense*, also wrote a pamphlet advocating for the emancipation of slaves and the abolition of slavery.

Thomas Jefferson included strong language against the slave trade in the original draft of the Declaration of Independence. However, this section was removed by the other delegates. The fact that Jefferson included this is interesting as he owned hundreds of slaves. Jefferson also signed the Act Prohibiting Importation of Slaves, which did exactly what it sounds like.

During the War of 1812, the British welcomed runaway slaves who would enlist in the British military. The Treaty of Ghent specified that all of these slaves were to be returned to their American owners; but more than ten years later, after no slaves were returned, Britain compensated the slave owners, hoping to make the issue go away. Many people recognized the problems of slavery; however, it took a civil war and the loss of thousands of lives to end the injustice of slavery.

Remarkable Remark

"What I do about slavery, and the colored race I do because I believe it helps to save the Union; and what I forbear, I forbear because I do *not* believe it would help to save the Union."

—*A. Lincoln*

Exciting Entry

On this day in 1928, Fats Domino was born. He became popular as a rhythm and blues (R&B) performer and later as a rock and roll star. His recordings were popular, selling roughly sixty-five million copies.

Prominent Passing

On this day in 1870, Wyatt Outlaw died. Following the Civil War, he became a town constable. The Klan staunchly opposed him and eventually hung him. His death sparked racial violence in the months to follow.

 **"UNBOUGHT AND UNBOSSED"**

Exciting Entry

On this day in 1897, Marian Anderson was born. She was a singer who saw support from Eleanor Roosevelt. She became world famous for her performance to a 75,000-person crowd at the Lincoln Memorial.

Prominent Passing

On this day in 1962, Willie Best died. Best was a talented, small time actor, best known for his character "Sleep 'n' Eat." He appeared in roughly 120 movies and eventually died of cancer.

Shirley Chisholm was the first black female to become a member of Congress, to seek the Democratic presidential nomination, and to run for president as a part of a major political party.

Chisholm was born in Brooklyn, New York. During the Great Depression, Chisholm and her sisters were sent to Barbados, where her mother was from, to live with their grandmother. While in Barbados, she attended a one-room schoolhouse and picked up a slight British accent.

Chisholm began her career as a teacher. Teaching remained her occupation until 1964, after which she became involved in New York City politics. She was elected as a representative of New York in 1968 and would serve seven terms in Congress. During this time, she pushed for greater funding for inner cities and for more government involvement in education. Chisholm ran for president in 1972 and received fourth place in the voting for the Democratic nominee.

One event that happened during Chisholm's tenure was the assassination attempt on Alabama Governor George Wallace, who had been known for promoting segregation. Chisholm visited Wallace while he was in the hospital, and a unique friendship was formed. When Chisholm tried to pass a bill in Congress on minimum wage, it was Wallace who helped rally Southern representatives to vote in favor of the bill.

THE WORLD'S GREATEST CONTRALTO

Marian Anderson was an accomplished American singer who did much to break down racial barriers.

As a child, Anderson demonstrated much natural vocal talent despite having no formal training. She grew up singing in her church's choir, capable of singing parts for just about any of the voices. Members of the congregation were able to send her for a year to a music school by combining their funds.

Despite the fact that numerous events declined to feature her because of her race, Anderson toured many Southern college campuses, performed with the Philadelphia Symphony, and had many successful European tours in the 1930s. She is largely regarded as the world's greatest contralto.

Anderson's most famous performance was in 1939 at the Lincoln Memorial. She had tried to procure the Constitution Hall but was rejected by its managers, the Daughters of the American Revolution (DAR). Eleanor Roosevelt and others resigned from the DAR and helped arrange for Anderson to sing at the Lincoln Memorial. She drew an audience of over 75,000 for her Easter Sunday performance.

Marian Anderson received the Presidential Medal of Freedom from President Lyndon Johnson in addition to many honorary degrees from schools around the country. She helped pave the way for black Americans to be recognized for their artistic ability and achieve distinction.

Remarkable Remark

"If one only searched one's heart one would know that none of us is responsible for the complexion of his skin, and that we could not change it…and many of us don't wish to."
—Marian Anderson

Exciting Entry

On this day in 1945, Charles "Bubba" Smith was born. He played several seasons in the NFL but is best remembered for his acting. He played police officer Moses Hightower in the Police Academy movies.

Prominent Passing

On this day in 1968, Juanita Hall died. She was a famous actor and was the first black performer to win a Tony. She performed on Broadway, including in the original 1949 production, South Pacific.

SENATOR EDWARD BROOKE III

Remarkable Remark

"I felt that if a senator truly believed in racial separatism I could live with that, but it was increasingly evident that some…played on bigotry purely for political gain."

—E. Brooke III

Exciting Entry

On this day in 1840, William H. Carney was born. He was the first black recipient of the Medal of Honor for not letting the flag fall during a Civil War battle while sustaining many dangerous wounds.

Prominent Passing

On this day in 1940, Robert Abbott died. His newspaper, the Chicago Defender, was one of the most read black newspapers in the United States, and he was one of the country's first black self-made millionaires.

In 1966, Edward Brooke III became the first black man to be popularly elected to the US Senate.

Brooke joined the Army shortly after the Pearl Harbor attack. He became a distinguished soldier while serving in Italy, earning a Bronze Star Medal. After returning home, he began a carrier in law and became involved in Massachusetts politics shortly after. His three bids at office failed and he returned to law.

Encouraged by several of his peers, Brooke re-entered politics, and in 1962, was elected as the attorney general for Massachusetts, becoming the first black state attorney general in the United States. He won his US Senate bid in 1966.

As a Republican senator, he was, as he called himself, a "creative Republican." He was the first Republican to call for President Nixon's resignation and spoke against President Ford when he pardoned Nixon. His bid for re-election in 1978 met with failure as he and his wife Remigia went through a bitter divorce, and he was accused of financial misconduct.

Brooke was diagnosed with breast cancer in 2002 and returned to the public spotlight to raise awareness of male breast cancer. President George W. Bush awarded Brooke the Presidential Medal of Freedom in 2004, and Brooke's biography *Bridging the Divide: My Life* was released in 2007. He passed away at his home in Coral Gables, Florida, in January 2015.

WOMEN'S HISTORY MONTH

For millennia, women have played an important role in history. While many of their accomplishments were ignored or attributed to others, many of today's modern conveniences would not be possible without their genius. Queens, presidents, first ladies, congresswomen, explorers, inventors, and many other professions have changed the world for the better.

In 1981, Congress passed a law authorizing the president to proclaim the week beginning with March 7, 1982, as "Women's History Week." Over the next five years, Congress passed joint resolutions authorizing a week in March to be set aside in honor of women. In 1987, Congress passed a law making March of 1987 "Women's History Month." It is for this reason that we honor thousands of women in the United States and across the globe. However, women and their accomplishments should not be recognized just in the month of March; their accomplishments should be recognized year round. Many women will never be recognized for their work, even though many women change the world for better. It is to these unsung heroes that this Women's History Month is dedicated.

March 1

HATSHEPSUT

Exciting Entry
On this day in 1868, Alaska P. Davidson was born. Davidson was the FBI's first female special agent, serving from 1922 to 1924. She left because of J. Edgar Hoover's plan to "clean house" within the FBI.

Prominent Passing
On this day in 1865, Anna Pavlovna of Russia died. She was a well-educated royal and even declined Napoleon Bonaparte's offer of marriage. She would go on to become Queen of Netherlands through marriage.

Sometime around 1504 B.C., Pharaoh Thutmose I had a daughter named Hatshepsut and a son by a secondary wife named Thutmose II.

Thutmose II was married to his half-sister Hatshepsut when she was around twelve years old. When Thutmose I died, his son Thutmose II began to reign with Hatshepsut as queen. Thutmose II died young, and his half-son Thutmose III became ruler, with Hatshepsut acting as regent.

However, Hatshepsut soon took control over the entire Egyptian Empire. Many historians believe she took over as pharaoh from Thutmose III because of infighting and in order to retain the throne for him.

Regardless, she was a powerful and successful pharaoh. She built roads, buildings, and many monuments. Her greatest building project was the large temple at Deir el-Bahri. She also successfully traded goods from her kingdom with others, bringing many exquisite items back to Egypt. She had many statues and drawings depicting her as a male pharaoh, but she retained her female identity within the carvings by signifying in different ways that she was a female.

Hatshepsut died sometime around 1458 B.C. and was buried in the Valley of the Kings. Thutmose III officially became pharaoh after Hatshepsut's death and erased most references to her in an effort to legitimize his reign. Her story was not uncovered until the 1800s.

CLEOPATRA

Perhaps the best-known woman from ancient times, Cleopatra was the powerful ruler of Egypt. Born around 70 B.C., she became the dominant co-ruler of Egypt in 51 B.C., but was soon forced to flee.

Cleopatra allied herself with Julius Caesar in an effort to regain her power and to retake the land that her ancestors had previously controlled. Cleopatra eventually regained her throne, and around 47 B.C., she had a son by Julius Caesar named Ptolemy Caesar. Cleopatra visited Rome and, according to some accounts, was actually in Rome when Julius Caesar was murdered.

Following Julius Caesar's death, Mark Antony and Octavian vied for power. Cleopatra, who had mesmerized Mark Antony, sided with him in his power grab. Antony needed the wealth of Cleopatra's kingdom to fund his military campaigns, while Cleopatra needed Antony's position of authority to regain parts of her ancestors' land that she had lost.

After Mark Antony's failed campaign, he returned to Egypt, ignored Octavian's claim to the throne, and proclaimed one of Cleopatra's sons the true heir to the throne, and Cleopatra queen. However, Octavian opposed this move and in the ensuing battles, Mark Antony and later Cleopatra took their own lives. Cleopatra was a scholar, scientist, and powerful world leader who shaped much of the ancient Roman world into what we know today.

Remarkable Remark

"She [Cleopatra] was one of the most dynamic figures the world has ever seen. And I don't think that's an exaggeration."
—*Joann Fletcher*

Exciting Entry

On this day in 1860, Susanna Salter was born. Salter was a prohibitionist and was jokingly nominated to run for mayor of Argonia, Kansas, by some men. She was elected the town's mayor with over 60% of the votes.

Prominent Passing

On this day in 1945, Emily Carr died. Carr was a prominent Canadian painter. She took trips to British Columbian Indian villages, where she became famous for her Indian and landscape paintings.

March 3

VIRGIN MARY

Exciting Entry

On this day in 1893, Beatrice Wood was born. Wood's art was influenced by the Dada movement and Eastern religion. She became well known in the art world for her unusual style of ceramic pottery.

Prominent Passing

On this day in 1966, Alice Pearce died. She was an American actress who was best known for her role on the series *Bewitched*. She also performed with Fred Astaire, Ed Sullivan, and Jerry Lewis.

Perhaps no other woman is as respected and honored as Mary, the mother of vJesus Christ. She is honored in Catholic, Muslim, and Protestant writings and is acknowledged and referred to in Jewish and Far Eastern religions.

Mary lived in Israel during the time of the Roman Empire. Little is known of her actual life apart from the Bible and tradition. Those testimonies inform us that Mary's parents were Joachim and Anne; she lived in Nazareth; had her son, Jesus, in Bethlehem; lived in Egypt for a time; traveled yearly to Jerusalem; attended a wedding in Cana; and traveled around Israel during the ministry of her son, Jesus Christ.

We also know that she had several other children, was most likely a widow by the time Jesus died, and possibly died either in the city of Ephesus or Jerusalem.

While little is known of her actual life, it was following her death and throughout the Middle Ages that the Virgin Mary became prominent in Christian teaching. The Catholic church believes in the assumption of Mary, or her being taken up into heaven, which is celebrated on August 15. Mary's assumed birthday, on September 8 has been celebrated as a feast day since around the seventh century. Mary is also held as the patron saint of all humanity. Whether all recognition given to Mary by the Catholic church is warranted, she does indeed stand out as deserving honor as one chosen by God.

March 4   EMPRESS THEODORA

When the Roman Empire became too big to effectively rule, it was split into the Roman empire and the Byzantine Empire. The Byzantine Empire lasted roughly a thousand years beyond the Roman Empire and was ruled by several famous rulers, including Justinian I and his wife Theodora.

Born sometime around A.D. 497, Theodora would become the most influential woman in the history of the Byzantine Empire. As a young woman, she was an actress and lived a scandalous lifestyle. However, she eventually abandoned her scandalous lifestyle, became religious, and made her living as a wool spinner in Constantinople.

She eventually met Justinian, and her beauty and intellect caught his eye. They were married after a special law was passed allowing them to do so. When Justinian became emperor, Theodora was proclaimed his empress. Empress Theodora was intelligent and, to some extent, ruled the empire. She received dignitaries, helped to pass numerous laws, and convinced her husband to remain in Constantinople and fight during a revolt.

Remarkable Remark
"As to the belief that a woman ought not to be daring among men or to assert herself boldly…I consider that the present…[revolt] does not permit us to discuss [it]."
—*Theodora*

Exciting Entry
On this day in 1781, Rebecca Gratz was born. She was a Jewish American philanthropist who helped found and run several charitable organizations. She also promoted religious education for the Jews.

Prominent Passing
On this day in 1986, Elizabeth Smart died. Smart's work *By Grand Central Station I Sat Down and Wept*, which gained her international fame, was based on her relationship with a married poet.

Both Empress Theodora and her husband held Christian beliefs, and Theodora helped pass legislation in support of women socially and politically. Today, Empress Theodora is often overlooked, but her influence shaped Eastern Europe and the Middle East for centuries.

 **5**

JOAN OF ARC

Exciting Entry

On this day in 1897, Madame Chiang Kai-shek was born. She was a prominent figure in Chinese and later Taiwanese politics. She was also the first Chinese person to address a joint session of Congress.

Prominent Passing

On this day in 1966, Anna Akhmatova died. A Russian poet, her poetry was suppressed by Communists. Her works were eventually fully published, and she was one of the greatest female Russian poets.

During the Middle Ages, thousands of peasants were born and died without any recognition. However, the occasional peasant made a name for himself and was remembered throughout history. Perhaps the best known of these exceptions was the "Maid of Orléans," Joan of Arc.

Joan was never taught to read and write, but she was instilled with the beliefs of the Catholic church and had an almost fanatical piety. She claimed to have visions and direct contact with deceased saints.

At the time, the French crown was in dispute between France and England, and in 1429, Joan was granted an audience before Charles, the French heir to the crown. Joan promised to defeat the English coalition and to help crown him the king of France. Charles reluctantly agreed, and Joan prepared to fight. Her most prominent victory was at Orléans, which was besieged by the English. Over the course of several days, Joan of Arc defeated the English coalition in several battles, and Charles was eventually crowned king.

Joan of Arc later was captured, tried, and eventually burned at the stake, but roughly twenty years after her death, Joan of Arc was vindicated. She was later canonized by the Catholic church. The Maid of Orléans proved that anyone could be a hero, regardless of their situation.

March **6**

QUEEN ISABEL

Queen Isabel I is perhaps best known as one of the royals who sponsored Christopher Columbus's voyages to the New World. However, she was also an extremely powerful European monarch.

Isabel was born in 1451 and was well educated, learning directly from many university scholars. Isabel married Ferdinand of Aragon and had the help of a later pope to confirm the marriage.

Following her father's and brothers' deaths, Isabel was named queen of Castile. Her and her husband served as king and queen over Aragon and Castile, uniting them into Spain in 1469. Many scholars consider Isabel to have been far more powerful than Ferdinand and to be one of the most powerful female rulers of all time.

The monarchs began the Spanish Inquisition, which was intended to rid their country of those who opposed the Catholic church. For their work, they became known as the "Catholic Monarchs," and Isabel became well known as Isabel the Catholic. The monarchs also defeated the Moors ending the *Reconquista*.

Remarkable Remark
"This queen of Spain, called Isabella, has had no equal on this earth for 500 years."
—*Unknown visitor on observing Queen Isabel*

Exciting Entry
On this day in 1806, Elizabeth Barrett Browning was born. She was a popular American poet who married another famous poet, Robert Browning. Her works attacked slavery and promoted feminism.

Prominent Passing
On this day in 1888, Louisa May Alcott died. She was a volunteer nurse during the Civil War and went on to become a famous writer. Her best-known works were *Little Women, Little Men,* and *Jo's Boys.*

The monarchs did support the exploration of Christopher Columbus, but the story of Isabel offering her crown jewels to support the trip is only a legend. When Indian slaves were brought back to Spain, Isabel ordered them to be set free. Isabel was a patron of religious, educational, and artistic endeavors until her death in 1504.

March **7**

QUEEN ELIZABETH I

Exciting Entry
On this day in A.D. 149, Lucilla was born. She was the daughter of Marcus Aurelius. She was banished and executed after being implicated in a plot to kill Commodus, her brother and then Roman emperor.

Prominent Passing
On this day in 1913, Emily Pauline Johnson died. Johnson was part Mohawk and often published her poetry under her Indian name Tekahionwake. Her poems exemplified the rich heritage of her tribe.

Perhaps the most powerful woman of her time, Queen Elizabeth I was one of England's greatest and most successful monarchs.

Elizabeth was born in 1533 and had no early expectations to be a ruler. However, following several deaths and escaping a plot to execute her, Elizabeth was crowned queen of England in 1558.

While Elizabeth worked to strengthen the position and doctrines of the Church of England, she was willing to compromise on certain religious ideas, possibly saving her country from religious wars like the ones in Europe.

Many explorers made a name for themselves during her reign, including Sir Walter Raleigh and Sir Francis Drake. During her reign, King Philip II's Spanish Armada was defeated, and exploration of the New World continued. Her reign also allowed many forms of fine arts to flourish, including the works of William Shakespeare. Her reputation led to her nicknames "Good Queen Bess" and "The Virgin Queen," from which the Virginia colony got its name.

However, not all was sunshine and roses. Many Roman Catholic rulers and radicals tried to attack England and to take Elizabeth I's life—the best known being Mary, Queen of Scots, who was eventually executed. The country was also plagued by high prices, debt, and economic depression. However, Queen Elizabeth I's reign was one of glory for her country.

MARY EDWARD WALKER

In American history, there have been over 3,500 Medals of Honor awarded for bravery. However, there has only been one female recipient—Mary Edward Walker.

Mary Edward Walker worked as a nurse in the beginning of the American Civil War but became the army's first female surgeon. She was captured by the Confederacy while tending to sick across enemy lines and was declared a spy. Walker was held as a prisoner of war for roughly four months before being released.

After the war ended, Walker was awarded the Medal of Honor by Andrew Johnson on November 11, 1865. In 1917, the Army changed the eligibility criteria to receive the Medal of Honor, and over nine hundred people lost their awards. This included Walker, who refused to return her medal and continued to wear her medal until she died two years later. During her lifetime, she was an ardent abolitionist, prohibitionist, she was against tobacco use, and she was an early advocate of women's rights. In 1977, the Army reversed their decision and returned the Medal of Honor to her.

Remarkable Remark

"[Walker] knew Governors, Senators, Generals, Actors…and practically all of the famous people of her day…Publicity was sweet to her, she was in the public eye and the press continually."

—Fred P. Wright

Exciting Entry

On this day in 1839, Josephine Cochrane was born. She invented the first practical dishwasher and displayed it at the Chicago World's Fair. It was originally used in hotels and large restaurants.

Prominent Passing

On this day in 2018, Kate Wilhelm died. She was a science fiction and mystery writer who wrote over forty books in her six-decade career. She was inducted into the Science Fiction Hall of Fame in 2003.

Walker became president of the National Dress Reform Association in 1866. She often dressed as a man, including the then popular top hat. She toured the United States and Europe discussing women's rights, dress reform, health, and temperance issues. Mary Edward Walker was honored for her years of service with a stamp in 1982.

WOMEN AND PROHIBITION

Exciting Entry
On this day in 1839,
Phoebe Knapp was
born. Knapp was good
friends with blind hymn
writer Fanny Crosby
and went on to write
the tunes to over 500
hymns, including Cros-
by's "Blessed Assurance."

Prominent Passing
On this day in 1947, Carrie
Catt died. Catt was a
devout women's rights
activist and led the Na-
tional American Woman
Suffrage Association
(NAWSA). Her work led
to the ratifying of the
Nineteenth Amendment.

For decades before the Eighteenth Amendment, people across the United States fought against liquor. One of the driving forces, outside of evangelical preachers, were women.

Prior to the Civil War, there were many women's organizations promoting temperance, but most focused on other issues during the Civil War. However, by the 1870s, the nation was healing, and temperance once again became a prominent issue. In 1874, the Women's Christian Temperance Union was founded to promote temperance. The women's efforts were rewarded, and Prohibition was in effect from 1920 to 1933.

Many of the more radical supporters of Prohibition tried to have the Bible rewritten to remove all references to alcohol. During Prohibition, these temperance activists hired a scholar to rewrite the Bible so that it "agreed" with their beliefs. In contrast to those prohibitionists, following the repeal of Prohibition in 1933, the first legal bottle of beer produced by Washington's Abner Drury Brewery was delivered to President Roosevelt at the White House.

During Prohibition, speakeasies, places one could buy illegal liquor, became popular. Amazingly, several of these speakeasies are still in operation today, including several in New York. While they have undergone renovations and change, much of their interior design and drink selection remains unchanged.

POCAHONTAS

Pocahontas is a somewhat controversial figure in American history, mainly because not much research was done on her until recent years, and most of what people "know" of her life comes from cartoons.

Pocahontas was not her real name. Her private name was Matoaka, while "Pocahontas" could mean either "playful one" or "ill-behaved child." While Pocahontas and John Smith did know each other, Pocahontas actually married the English tobacco planter John Rolfe.

Pocahontas's marriage to John Rolfe helped to continue the peace between the Native Americans and the English colonists. She had met Rolfe while being held captive as a bargaining chip of the English leaders as they sought a permanent peace with her father, "Wahunsenacawh," or Powhatan.

The following year, Pocahontas gave birth to Thomas Rolfe, their first child. He went on to be a leading citizen in the now-flourishing Jamestown colony. For the next two years, Pocahontas and Rolfe traveled to and lived in England. The couple even had the chance to visit the court of King James I.

Remarkable Remark

"Master John Rolfe, an honest Gentleman, and of good behavior, had beene in love with Pocahontas, and she with him."
—John Smith on Rolfe and Pocahontas

Exciting Entry

On this day in 1847, Kate Sheppard was born. Sheppard lived in New Zealand and was a women's rights activist. She helped convince New Zealand's Parliament to grant women the right to vote in 1893.

Prominent Passing

On this day in 1913, Harriet Tubman died. Tubman is best remembered as a conductor for the Underground Railroad. She led some seventy people to freedom and had a forty thousand dollar reward for her capture.

As they were preparing to head back to Virginia in 1617, Pocahontas died. Five years later, John Rolfe also died; however, he died not from smallpox as Pocahontas did, but from an Indian massacre. A monument to Pocahontas stands in England where she died while on her way back to her home.

GRACE O'MALLEY

Sometime around 1530, Grace O'Malley was born. Largely forgotten to history, her life was a testament of what a woman could accomplish regardless of the social expectations of the time.

Grace O'Malley was a member of a powerful Irish clan who was well-known for its pirating of ships and trading with foreign countries. Grace, although a woman in the male-dominated sixteenth century, became a prominent pirate. She was known for her stubbornness and leadership abilities, and most of her crew willingly followed her lead.

O'Malley's trading ships often pirated the English's ships, but she offered the English several hundred fighting men to appease their anger. Grace O'Malley's trading took her to ports throughout Europe and continued to grow her wealth, power, and prestige. Although on the high seas constantly trading and fighting, Grace O'Malley had several children.

O'Malley was a pirate queen, and at the height of her power, she commanded hundreds of men and many ships. She met and spoke in Latin with Queen Elizabeth I, perhaps the only contemporary woman with more power than Grace. Supposedly, O'Malley refused to bow and accept a title of nobility because they were equals. Grace O'Malley died in 1603 and proved that women can beat social norms and become a legend in their own unique way.

SOPHIE GERMAIN

Sophie Germain was born into a wealthy middle-class French family in 1776 and became famous for her work as an accomplished mathematician.

While her parents were opposed to Germain's constant studying, Germain continued to learn geometry, mathematics, and foreign languages. She continued her education by borrowing university professors' lecture notes, a common practice at the time. She used the male pseudonym "M. le Blanc" to obtain the notes and submit comments. She also used a male pseudonym in an effort to have her work and suggestions taken seriously at a time when a woman's contribution would not be.

Under her fake name, she corresponded and collaborated with famous mathematicians Joseph-Fouis Lagrange and Carl Friedrich Gauss, and both continued to work with her after finding out she was a woman. She also studied number theory and made advancements in the understanding of Fermat's Last Theorem.

When the French Academy of Sciences hosted a competition on vibration, Germain won the award (after several submissions). Sadly, most of the academic community avoided her because she was a woman, and only a few saw her brilliance during her lifetime. Sophie Germain's contributions included the fields of of acoustics, elasticity, and number theory.

Remarkable Remark
"She proved to the world that even a woman can accomplish something worth while…and for that reason would have well deserved an honorary degree."
—*Carl Gauss*

Exciting Entry
On this day in 1862, Jane Delano was born. She was a nurse who helped combat yellow fever in Jacksonville, Florida. She led part of the Red Cross and prepared over twenty thousand nurses for World War I.

Prominent Passing
On this day in 1978, Theresa Blanchard died. Blanchard was a prominent figure skater who helped train other skaters. She earned over thirty medals in her career, including a bronze medal at the Olympics.

SALEM WITCH TRIAL

March 13

Remarkable Remark

"I am as innocent as the child unborn.... I am innocent I know nothing of it. I am no witch I know not what a witch is."

—Bridget Bishop

Exciting Entry

On this day in 1798, Abigail Fillmore was born. Fillmore was the last of the first ladies to be born in the 1700s. She successfully lobbied Congress to appropriate money to build a White House library.

Prominent Passing

On this day in 1906, Susan B. Anthony died. President Carter signed the Susan B. Anthony Dollar Coin Act in honor of her women's rights activity. The coin is remembered for its oddly-shaped edges.

Of all the events during America's colonial era, none perhaps are as intriguing as the Salem Witch Trials, held from 1692 to 1693.

While there were numerous factors that caused the hysteria, the overall theme was quarreling, which the Puritans believed was the work of the Devil. When the pastor's daughter and niece began having "fits," they were again blamed on the Devil.

The two young girls were heavily influenced to blame the people responsible, and the girls ultimately blamed three women: a slave, a beggar, and an old, poor woman. While two claimed innocence, the slave girl confessed, and all three were placed in jail.

In the ensuing chaos and paranoia, dozens of people from around the Salem area were questioned. In May of 1692, a special court was established to begin condemning the supposed witches. The first woman to be killed was Bridget Bishop, who was hanged. While the esteemed minister Cotton Mather cautioned the court, his warning went unheeded. The trials were not stopped until the governor's wife was questioned as a witch.

Over two hundred people were accused of practicing witchcraft, while nineteen were hanged, an old man was pressed to death by heavy stones, and several died in prison. In 1702, the trials were declared unlawful, and the heirs of those who died were paid restitution in 1711. The state of Massachusetts would not formally apologize until 1957.

March 14   **FAMOUS FIRST LADIES**

In the almost 250 years of US history, Americans have had 45 presidents. The saying "Behind every great man is a greater woman" has certainly applied more than once during this time.

Martha Washington was the first first lady and the first presidential wife to appear on a US postage stamp. Dolley Madison as a former first lady was given an honorary seat to attend sessions of Congress. John Tyler's first wife was the first wife to die in the White House and Tyler's second wife became the first first lady to be photographed.

Eliza Johnson, Andrew Johnson's wife, taught her husband how to spell properly, and Lucy Hayes was the first to ban alcohol in the White House. Ida McKinley quite possibly successfully lobbied her husband to hold onto the Philippines after the Spanish-American War, and Eleanor Roosevelt was the first first lady to hold regular press conferences. Pat Nixon started White House tours for the blind and deaf, and Michelle Obama was the first African American first lady.

Remarkable Remark

"These women…are important…because of the contributions they have made to various social causes. The impact of the First Ladies has never been very well-publicized."
—Patricia Krider

Exciting Entry

On this day in 1997, Simone Biles was born. Biles is one of the most talented Olympic gymnasts of all time and an important world figure because of her athletic ability. She also enjoys history and reading.

Prominent Passing

On this day in 1977, Fannie Lou Hamer died. Hamer was a civil rights activist who tried to integrate the Democratic Party in Mississippi. She died at the age of fifty-nine after losing her battle with cancer.

Each of the first ladies shaped the presidency in her own way. Each promoted different causes for the general good of the country in thier own unique way. While no woman has ever held the office of president, many have campaigned, and in the future, America will most likely have its first woman president.

MARIE ANTOINETTE

Exciting Entry

On this day in 1838, Alice Cunningham Fletcher was born. Fletcher studied Indian tribes across the United States and worked tirelessly for fair treatment of the tribes she studied and wrote about.

Prominent Passing

On this day in 2017, Jackie Pung died. She was a prominent female golfer who earned the title "Hawaii's First Lady of Golf" and was the first female from Hawaii to win a golf national championship.

In 1775, Marie Antoinette was born. One of the most captivating women of her day, she is best known for something she never said.

The French people were strongly against the monarchy, and the anti-royal propaganda machine capitalized on the people's hatred. Perhaps the best-known phrase from the revolution was when Antoinette heard that the people could not afford to buy bread. It is often reported that she said, "*Qu'ils mangent de la brioche*," or, "Let them eat cake."

While the supposed statement made the queen a hated person in France, more recent historians believe a statement like that would be highly uncharacteristic of the philanthropic Antoinette. Another reason is that several writings from before Antoinette was queen mentioned a story and saying very similar to the supposed comment. One version uses the Spanish princess Marie-Thérèse, who married King Louis XIV and suggested that the French people eat the crust of the pâté.

In 1766, Jean-Jacques Rousseau wrote about a powerful princess who made the comment (Marie Antoinette was only ten at the time). Although it was most certainly not Marie Antoinette who said it, the French Revolution became violent, and Antoinette eventually lost her head. In her honor, the first permanent US settlement on the Northwest Territory was named after her: Marietta, Ohio.

 **March 16** **AMERICAN SUFFRAGE**

In the United States it took roughly 150 years before women could actively participate in politics.

In 1848, the first women's rights convention was held at Seneca Falls, New York. Two years later, the first National Women's Rights Convention was held in Massachusetts, with over one thousand members. In 1869, the suffragist movement split over the method of gaining the vote.

Women like Susan B. Anthony and Elizabeth Cady Stanton wanted to gain the vote through a constitutional amendment, while others like Lucy Stone and Henry Blackwell wanted to gain the vote through state constitutions.

In 1872, Susan B. Anthony was arrested for voting in Ulysses Grant's election. In 1890, the National American Woman Suffrage Association was formed and worked to gain state approval for suffrage. Over the next two decades, several states and territories granted women the right to vote. In 1920, the Nineteenth Amendment was ratified.

Remarkable Remark
"There never will be complete equality until women themselves help to make laws and elect lawmakers."
—Susan B. Anthony

Exciting Entry
On this day in 1799, Anna Atkins was born. A botanist, she was best known for using a photographic process called cyanotype in her work. She learned the process from her friend Sir John Herschel.

Prominent Passing
On this day in 1940, Selma Lagerlöf died. She is considered to be one of modern day's best storywriters, and in 1909, became the first woman and Swedish writer to win a Nobel Prize in Literature.

Women's suffrage was led by people like Susan B. Anthony, Alice Paul, Ida B. Wells, and Frederick Douglass, who all recognized the importance of freedom and equality for all, regardless of gender.

 **March 17**

FLORENCE NIGHTINGALE

Remarkable Remark
"I have had a larger responsibility of human lives than ever man or woman had before. And I attribute my success to this: —*I never gave or took an excuse.*"
— *Florence Nightingale*

Exciting Entry
On this day in 1873, Margaret Bondfield was born. Although she had little formal education, she became a trade-union leader and eventually became the first female cabinet minister in Great Britain.

Prominent Passing
On this day in 1956, Irène Curie died. Irène was the daughter of Pierre and Marie Curie who went on to win the Nobel Prize in Chemistry in 1935. She also advanced women's social and academic causes.

In 1820, Florence Nightingale was born. Although born into a wealthy British family, she felt called to help the wounded as a nurse.

She was well educated but wanted to be a nurse, a profession often looked down upon by wealthy elites. Her parents eventually supported her decision, and she trained for several months in Germany.

During the Crimean War, the British were overwhelmed by the numbers of casualtie. The government asked Nightingale to lead a group of nurses to the battle front to help with the wounded. While the male doctors did not want their help initially, when the casualties continued to grow, they asked for the nurses' help. With the help of Florence Nightingale and the other nurses, the mortality rate dropped over 30%. Florence Nightingale often visited the soldiers at night and was affectionately called "the Lady with the Lamp" by the soldiers.

After the war, Nightingale continued to improve hospital conditions, presented her work to the British king and queen, and became the first female elected to the Royal Statistical Society. Her writing and work promoted safer nursing practices and better health conditions. Nightingale died in 1910 at the age of ninety. Two years later, the International Committee of the Red Cross created the Florence Nightingale Medal, given to nurses who work with veterans of war and promote public health.

LOUISA MAY ALCOTT

In 1832, Louisa May Alcott was born. She was a prolific author and is one of the most famous female authors.

Born to a Pennsylvanian family, her parents were a part of the then-popular Transcendentalist movement. She studied under famous men like Henry David Thoreau, Ralph Waldo Emerson, and Nathaniel Hawthorne. Her parents' religious views and the beliefs of the men she studied under greatly influenced her.

In 1854, her first book was published. Alcott served as a Union nurse during the Civil War until she contracted typhoid. Her time in the Civil War led to her novel *Hospital Sketches*, and many of her early works were under the name A. M. Barnard.

In 1868, her most famous work, *Little Women*, was published and was based on her childhood. Originally published in multiple segments, it was eventually published as one book. She quickly became famous, and a few years later, Alcott published *Little Men*.

Alcott's success and fame helped gain her recognition. She joined the growing suffrage movement, even contributing several works promoting women's rights. In 1875, Alcott attended the Women's Congress in Syracuse, New York and was the first woman to register to vote in Concord, Massachusetts. She died at the age of 56 and was buried on "Author's Ridge" near other literary greats in the Sleepy Hollow Cemetery in Concord.

Remarkable Remark
"Women have been called queens for a long time, but the kingdom given them isn't worth ruling."
—Louisa May Alcott

Exciting Entry
On this day in 1927, Lillian Vernon was born. Vernon built a successful catalog business in America, which became the first company owned by a woman to be listed on the American Stock Exchange.

Prominent Passing
On this day in 2019, Jerrie Cobb died. She was the first US female astronaut candidate, but because of her gender, she never went to space. She instead became a humanitarian pilot in the Amazon.

MARIE CURIE

Remarkable Remark
"I am one of those who believe with Nobel that mankind will derive more good than harm from the new discoveries."
—*Pierre Curie speaking on behalf of the couple*

Exciting Entry
On this day in 1894, Moms Mabley was born. Mabley was a popular black comedian who made a name for herself in Vaudeville. She was known for her comical facial expressions, outfits, and jokes.

Prominent Passing
On this day in 2017, Mary Maples Dunn died. She was a promoter for women's history and was the president of Smith College. She wanted to be remembered for making the Smith a more diverse college.

Marie Curie is one of the world's greatest scientist who became famous at a time when women were not acknowledged as scientists.

Born in Warsaw, Poland, Marie studied physics and mathematics in Paris. While there, Marie met Pierre Curie, a professor, and they got married in 1895. The couple worked together in the field of radioactivity, and in 1898, they announced their discovery of polonium, a new chemical element named after Marie's home country Poland.

A few months later, they again announced the discovery of another element, radium. In 1903, the Curies, along with another physicist, won the Nobel Prize in Physics. Sadly, Pierre's life was cut short when he was run over by a carriage. Marie Curie continued her research and became a teacher. Her continued work led her to winning another Nobel Prize but this time in chemistry.

Her work led to the further development of x-ray use, and she used her knowledge during WWI, even going to the front lines. Curie disliked public attention and never got much recognition in France. However, she received a royal welcome on her six-week US tour. She met with several prominent citizens, including President Harding, and received honors from many prominent universities. Marie Curie's death was caused from the years of high radiation exposure over her decades-long, groundbreaking career.

NANCY ASTOR

Few today recognize the name Nancy Astor, but her role in British politics was groundbreaking and unusual.

Born in Virginia in 1879, she grew up in a family that quickly gained wealth. In 1897, Nancy married Robert Shaw, but they divorced in 1903. Astor soon went to England and met millionaire Waldorf Astor on the journey. They eventually married in 1906 and lived in England.

In 1910, Waldorf won a seat in the House of Commons, where he served until 1919. Waldorf's father was a Lord, and following his death in 1919, Waldorf became a Lord and moved to serve in the House of Lords. Lady Nancy Astor then ran and successfully won the seat in Parliament vacated by her husband.

Nancy Astor became the first woman to take a seat in Parliament and remained the only woman until 1921. Lady Astor advocated for temperance, shorter working hours, and women's rights. During WWII, she was accused of being a Nazi sympathizer but quickly proved she was strongly pro-British. During the Battle of Britain, she visited her constituents and kept the morale up during the trying time.

She left Parliament in 1945 but remained a vocal social critic of both British and US politics as well as a vocal opponent of Communism. While no legislation is associated with her and she held no government post, Nancy Astor was a pioneer in British politics.

Remarkable Remark

"Lady Astor…[is] the World's most famous intellectual Clown and Pantaloon in one, and the charming Columbine of the capitalist pantomime."
—*Winston Churchill*

Exciting Entry

On this day in 1951, Tanya Boyd was born. She is an American actress who is best known for her role as Celeste Perrault from 1994 to 2007 in the daytime series *Days of Our Lives*, which began in 1965.

Prominent Passing

On this day in 2004, Juliana died. Juliana was the Netherlands' queen from 1948 to 1980, and kept a modest life, often seen shopping at the local supermarket. She voluntarily abdicated in 1980.

HELEN KELLER

Remarkable Remark

"Although the world is full of suffering, it is full also of the overcoming of it."
—*Helen Keller*

Exciting Entry

On this day in 1474, St. Angela Merici was born. She advocated for the Christian education of girls and founded the Ursuline Order to accomplish her goal. She was canonized in 1807 for her service.

Prominent Passing

On this day in 1992, Natalie Sleeth died. Sleeth was a music composer and wrote over 180 songs including the songs "Joy in the Morning," "In the Bulb there is a Flower," and "Hymn of Promise."

One of the most forgotten humanitarians from the twentieth century was also deaf and blind. Regardless of her impairments, Helen Keller achieved things many could only dream of.

Helen Keller was born in 1880 a healthy child; however, shortly before her second birthday, she came down with a serious illness that left her deaf and blind. Because of her illness, she had little education in her early years. Her family even asked for Alexander Graham Bell's help, as he worked with deaf people. Ultimately, Anne Sullivan would become Keller's mentor and lifelong teacher.

She continued her education for several years and even graduated from college with honors. Keller had also written two books prior to her graduation. Keller lived with Sullivan and her husband and became an advocate for women's suffrage, socialism, and pacifism during WWI. Keller also co-founded the American Civil Liberties Union (ACLU) in 1920, along with Jane Addams and other activists.

Keller became well known for her lecturing and advocacy for the blind, and she also toured military hospitals during WWII. Keller received several honorary doctorates from prestigious universities, met with several US presidents and foreign leaders, and received the Presidential Medal of Freedom in 1964. Keller passed away in 1968, but her life has been an inspiration for many since then.

March **22** MATA HARI

One of the most famous women from WWI is the spy Mata Hari, who is best known for something she never was.

Mata Hari was born in 1876 and lived in Indonesia after marrying a Dutch officer. However, they moved back to Europe and soon divorced. She decided to become a dancer and billed herself as a woman of Far Eastern descent.

Throughout Mata Hari's career, she captivated thousands across Europe and was acquainted with many powerful men and government officials. She was able to easily travel throughout Europe during WWI as her nation of birth, the Netherlands, was neutral.

However, Mata Hari was purposefully set up as a spy, likely to boost faltering French morale. While Mata Hari's lifestyle brought up many questions of loyalty and the possibility of espionage, no real evidence existed. In the resulting trial, she was accused of causing thousands of French deaths, although these claims were never substantiated and several pieces of evidence were changed. She was found guilty of espionage and was executed by firing squad.

Remarkable Remark
"She was led at daybreak from her cell in the Saint-Lazare prison to a waiting automobile and then rushed to the barracks where the firing squad awaited her."
—*Account of Hari's death*

Exciting Entry
On this day in 1928, Betty Callaway was born. Callaway was a British ice skating coach whose pupils won numerous national and international awards, including winning gold in the 1984 Winter Olympics.

Prominent Passing
On this day in 2018, Morgana King died. King was a well-known jazz singer, recording roughly twenty albums, but is best remembered for her role as Carmela Corleone in the first two *Godfather* movies.

Her shady, immoral lifestyle and mystique led most to begin thinking of her as a spy, yet no reliable information is known to exist that proves she really was a spy. The myth of Mata Hari as a spy remains to this day.

 **March 23**

AMELIA EARHART

One of the early pioneers of aviation was the female aviatrix, Amelia Earhart. Her accomplishments as a pilot, however, are often overshadowed by her mysterious disappearance.

Born in Kansas in 1897, Amelia grew up with little interest in flight. She served as a nurse during WWI, and during this time, Amelia's interest in flying began.

Throughout 1921, Earhart took flying lessons, bought her own plane, and earned her pilot's license. In 1922, she set an unofficial female altitude record. In 1928, Amelia became the first female passenger on a trans-Atlantic flight and quickly became a star. In 1929, Amelia Earhart helped found The Ninety-Nines, an organization for female pilots, and became the organization's first president.

In 1930, Earhart set the women's world flying speed record. In 1931, she married George Putnam. In 1932, Amelia Earhart became the first female to fly solo across the Atlantic Ocean, cementing her into aviation history and earning herself numerous awards from nations across the globe. In 1937, Earhart was on her round-world flight when she and her navigator suddenly disappeared, and she was declared legally dead in 1939. Her work in aviation led to numerous advances for women in the field of aviation and proved to the world that women could be some of the best pilots in the world.

MOTHER TERESA

In the city of Skopje in North Macedonia, Agnes Gonxha Bojaxhiu was born. Known for her work to the poor in India, she is one of the best-known women in the twentieth century.

Known world wide as Mother Teresa, she was called at an early age into the ministry. She eventually joined the Sisters of Loreto in India and taught at a high school in Calcutta for some fifteen years. In 1948, she received permission to work with the poverty-ridden people of Calcutta and soon opened a school for the poor.

In 1950, Mother Teresa received permission to found the order Missionaries of Charity, whose main goal was taking care of the poor and loving the unlovable. Today, the order works in countries around the globe. Mother Teresa continued helping the poor by educating them, feeding them, and providing medical services to them. Mother Teresa died in 1997, and the process of her becoming a Catholic saint began two years later. The Catholic church bestowed sainthood on Mother Teresa in 2016.

Remarkable Remark
"By blood and origin I am Albanian. My citizenship is Indian. I am a Catholic nun. As to my calling, I belong to the whole world. As to my heart, I belong entirely to the heart of Jesus."
—*Mother Teresa*

Exciting Entry
On this day in 1912, Dorothy Height was born. She was a civil and women's rights activist and sought progress for African American women. She was awarded the Presidential Medal of Freedom in 1994.

Prominent Passing
On this day in 1603, Elizabeth I died. During her reign, called the Elizabethan Period, the Church of England was restored, the Spanish Armada was defeated, and the East India Company was founded.

Throughout her decades of ministry, she helped thousands of people and earned over 120 awards, including the Nobel Peace Prize, in recognition of her dedication. Mother Teresa gained many enemies for her stance against divorce and abortion. While some are skeptical of her motives of service and the actual care she gave to those in need, many view her life of service as what one can accomplish when dedicated to a cause.

ELISABETH ELLIOT

Exciting Entry
On this day in 1942, Aretha Franklin was born. She was a popular religious, blues, and soul singer. Her talent earned her the moniker "Queen of Soul," and she sang at President Obama's inauguration.

Prominent Passing
On this day in 1917, Elizabeth Storrs Mead died. Mead taught at Andover Seminary and Oberlin College, and she later became the first non-alumni president of Mount Holyoke Seminary and College.

Elisabeth Elliot was one of the most captivating women of the late twentieth century and was known for her courageousness after her husband's death.

Elisabeth was born in 1926 and eventually attended Wheaton College with the goal of becoming a missionary and Bible translator. While there, she dated Jim Elliot; however, he believed he should remain single. Both went to Ecuador separately and were engaged and married in Ecuador soon after their arrival.

Jim's goal was to reach the unreached Auca tribe. Jim, along with four other missionaries, visited the Aucas, which had been receptive to earlier package drops and visits. However, on one visit, when the five men got out of their plane to visit, they were speared to death.

Life magazine honored the five missionaries' efforts, and soon after the loss of her husband, Elisabeth Elliot wrote *Through Gates of Splendor*. She continued to live in Ecuador and actually contacted and lived with the Auca tribe for two years. Through her missionary work, many Auca received the Lord as their Savior, including the man who had killed two of the missionaries. She eventually returned to the United States and was a major force for evangelism, touring the country and writing books for the next fifty years. Elisabeth Elliot's life proved to the world that a Christ-like forgiveness would always reap a rich reward.

March 26   FAMOUS ACTRESSES

Many women have made a name for themselves in acting; however, many actresses also made contributions as inventors as well.

In the late 2000s, Paula Abdul was granted a patent for a special microphone stand. This stand allowed performers to sway on the stand with ease while singing. Abdul is known for her singing and dancing and was an *American Idol* judge for several seasons.

In 1989, Christie Brinkley filed a patent for an educational toy that allowed young children to create and learn the letters of the alphabet. While mainly known for her modeling career, Brinkley used her idea to further the education of children.

In 1987, Jamie Lee Curtis filed a patent for a baby diaper that included a built-in compartment for baby wipes, cutting down on the hassle of needing multiple items for one diaper change. Curtis is a well-known actor and a mother of two.

In 1941, film actress Hedy Lamarr and a co-partner filed a patent for a communications device that stopped frequencies from being jammed. Lamaar's technology is used today in Wi-Fi, GPS, cellphones, and other technological devices.

Hedy Lamaar, Jamie Lee Curtis, Christie Brinkley, Paula Abdul, and other famous women proved that women could be multi-faceted in their careers.

Remarkable Remark

"Hope and curiosity about the future seemed better than guarantees. That's the way I was. The unknown was always so attractive to me…and still is."

—Hedy Lamarr

Exciting Entry

On this day in 1940, Nancy Pelosi was born. A Democrat politician, she has served in several positions in the House of Representatives. Up to 2019, she has served as Speaker of the House three times.

Prominent Passing

On this day in 1962, Augusta Savage died. As an artist, she sculpted during a period of intense racism against black Americans. She used her talent to gain support for more black Americans in art.

KALPANA CHAWLA

For centuries, women have made advancements in technology and science. However, one name that is mostly forgotten is Kalpana Chawla.

Kalpana Chawla was born in India in 1961. She excelled in school and earned her degree in aeronautical engineering in 1982. In an effort to further her education, she came to America, where she earned her masters from the University of Texas and her Ph.D. from the University of Colorado.

She went on to join NASA's research team, where she worked on power-lift computational fluid dynamics. She became an astronaut candidate in 1995 and went through a year of training. In 1997, she went into space aboard the space shuttle *Columbia,* which orbited the Earth 252 times while conducting many experiments.

In 2003, Kalpana again journeyed aboard the *Columbia* on another mission in space. After conducting several dozen experiments, the crew began their return to earth. However, on February 1, 2003, the space shuttle broke up on reentry, killing all on board the spacecraft. Throughout her brief yet successful life, Kalpana logged over thirty days in space and earned many awards. Kalpana Chawla's career proved to others that any person can achieve any goal he or she sets.

MARGARET THATCHER

Perhaps no other woman has influenced the United Kingdom or the world in the twentieth century as much as Margaret Thatcher.

Margaret Thatcher was born in 1925 to a shopkeeper and gained her education at Oxford University, where she became an early voice for British conservatism. She was elected as a conservative member of Parliament (MP) in 1959 and in 1970, and she was a member of the Cabinet as minister of education.

In 1979, the Conservative Party came into power, and Margaret Thatcher became the new prime minister. Thatcher was Great Britain's first female prime minister. Under her tenure, the economy began to improve, and she gained international recognition when she led the country to war against Argentina over the Falkland Islands.

In 1983, the Conservative Party won the election decisively, and Thatcher remained as Great Britain's prime minister. Thatcher continued her tenure by deregulating the economy and allowing even greater economic freedom. Margaret Thatcher also became well known as President Ronald Reagan's conservative counterpart against the Soviet Union. She stepped down as prime minister in 1990 and was appointed a life peerage in the House of Lords in 1992, earning her the title Baroness Thatcher of Kesteven. Thatcher proved that women could do great things in politics, and she helped pave the way for other woman leaders in governments.

Remarkable Remark
"You only win by being *for*...a free society with power well distributed amongst the citizens and *not* concentrated in the hands of the state."
—*Margaret Thatcher*

Exciting Entry
On this day in 1930, Amelia Rosselli was born. She was an Italian poet and is often considered one of the best post-WWII Italian writers. Her writing discussed the Cold War, racism, sexism, and WWII.

Prominent Passing
On this day in 1929, Katharine L. Bates died. She was a teacher at Wellesley College for several decades but is best remembered for her poem "America the Beautiful," which was eventually set to music.

GRACE HOPPER

Remarkable Remark

"If Wright is flight, and Edison is light, then Hopper is code."

—President Obama on Grace Hopper

Exciting Entry

On this day in 1954, Karen Quinlan was born. The courts allowed her parents to take her off life support after she fell into a coma. However, she lived ten more years on life support before she died.

Prominent Passing

On this day in 1683, Oshichi died. After attempting arson, Oshichi, at the age of sixteen, was burned at the stake as punishment. Following her death, her life was immortalized in several Japanese plays.

Women have made names for themselves through their many accomplishments. Grace Hopper is one of those women.

Born in 1906, Grace Hopper had a unique mathematical capability and love for learning and earned a Ph.D. in mathematics from Yale. In 1943, she left teaching to join the WAVES and worked as a researcher.

During her service, she helped work on an early computer called the Mark I, and she personally wrote a book on how computing machines operated. Following WWII, she remained in the naval reserves but became a computer science researcher. She helped create the UNIVAC I (an early computer), developed the first compiler, and helped develop an early computer language called COBOL. Hopper believed that computers, which at that time could fill a room, would soon fit on a desk.

Hopper was called back to active duty in 1967 and helped with computer programming languages. In 1973, she was promoted to captain and by 1985, she was made rear admiral. Following her retirement, Grace Hopper went back to teaching until her death in 1992. She earned numerous awards and accolades, including posthumously receiving the Presidential Medal of Freedom. While many do not realize how important her work was, Grace Hopper's foresight is a major reason why people everywhere today can use computers.

March **30**

BARBARA JORDAN

While those who know the name Barbara Jordan know her for her work in the Nixon impeachment hearings, few realize her extensive role in American politics.

Barbara Jordan was born in Houston in 1936 and aspired to become a lawyer. She graduated from college with honors and was known for her debating ability. Following college, she went on to get her law degree and was soon active in Texas politics. She became a Texas state senator in 1966.

Jordan was elected president pro tempore of the state senate and, because of her position, was able to serve as governor for a day. Following her time in the Texas senate, Jordan ran for Congress and won, becoming the first African American woman from the South to serve in the US House of Representatives.

In Congress, Jordan served in the House Judiciary Committee and gave the opening statement of the committee's Richard Nixon's impeachment hearings. She defended the proper use of the US Constitution, and Jordan became well known for her defense of the Constitution.

Jordan also advocated for women's rights. After retiring from Congress in 1979, she became a college professor. Her years of work earned her the Presidential Medal of Freedom in 1994. Her political work was groundbreaking and showed other minority women that they could also become a member of Congress.

Remarkable Remark

"My faith in the Constitution is whole…I am not going to sit here and be an idle spectator to the diminution, the subversion, the destruction of the Constitution."
—*Barbara Jordan*

Exciting Entry

On this day in 1888, Anna Nilsson was born. She was a famous silent-film star in the early 1900s, appearing in several dozen movies. Her last film appearance was in *Seven Brides for Seven Brothers*.

Prominent Passing

On this day in 2002, Queen Elizabeth, the Queen Mother, died. As a fourteen-year-old girl, she helped wounded soldiers in Britain during WWI and was in Buckingham Palace as queen when it was bombed in WWII.

 **MADELEINE ALBRIGHT**

Exciting Entry

On this day in 1929, Liz Claiborne was born. Claiborne was a fashion designer who helped create fashionable wardrobes to meet the needs for the new class of career and business-women going to work.

Prominent Passing

On this day in 1855, Charlotte Brontë died. Brontë's family was well known for their writing, and she herself was a popular writer. Her best-known work is her 1847 novel *Jane Eyre: An Autobiography*.

Of all the women who have played a part in US politics, perhaps no other woman has held as powerful a position as Madeleine Albright, the first woman US secretary of state.

Born in 1937 in Czechoslovakia, Madeleine and her family fled to England during WWII, returned to Czechoslovakia, and then made their way to America in 1948.

Madeleine studied political science in college and graduated with honors. She married her husband three days after receiving her diploma. They moved several times in the next few years, but Albright continued her studies and earned her Ph.D. in 1976. In the next few years, Albright got her first taste in politics as a Congressional assistant and later as NSA liaison to Congress.

Albright got divorced in 1982 and went on to teach at Georgetown University. When Bill Clinton won the presidency, he nominated Madeleine Albright as the ambassador to the UN. In 1996, President Clinton again nominated Albright, but this time it was for secretary of state. In 1997, Albright, after being unanimously confirmed by the Senate, was sworn in. A key moment in her tenure was when she visited North Korea in 2000, becoming the first high-level US official to visit the totalitarian country. Madeleine Albright's role as secretary of state paved the way for other women to take that role and to pursue the presidency.

THE CIVIL WAR

When spectators sat on the hills surrounding the First Battle of Bull Run, no one expected that it would lead to thousands dying within the next four years. However, as the battle began, the spectators quickly realized the realities of war and soon had to flee for safety. Over the next four years, nearly 10,500 military actions occurred and made places like Vicksburg, Gettysburg, Antietam, and Appomattox Court House well-known names.

However, the war spanned from Vermont to California and even effected places like Australia, Hawaii, and Russian Alaska. The war determined whether slavery would be a settled institution and if the state was subservient to the national government. To many, the Civil War incites the same emotions that those who served felt. Over seventy thousand books have been written specifically on the Civil War; however, we hope that this month you learn stories, facts, and people you may not have previously known.

April 1

THE CANING OF CHARLES SUMNER

Exciting Entry

On this day in 1823, Confederate general Simon Bolivar Buckner was born. Buckner fought at the battles of Perryville and Chickamauga and became Kentucky's governor after the Civil War ended.

Prominent Passing

On this day in 1865, Union general Frederic Winthrop died. He was one of the last Union officers to die in the Civil War, and his claim to fame was his famous ancestor, Governor John Winthrop.

While many think of the Civil War as starting at Fort Sumter, several fights across the country prior to the war broke out. One such fight was in Congress in 1856.

Charles Sumner, an antislavery senator, was speaking on the issue of Kansas being admitted to the Union when he verbally attacked Democrat Senators Stephen Douglass of Illinois and Andrew Butler of South Carolina.

While Butler was not there the day he was verbally attacked, his friend and distant relative, South Carolina Representative Preston Brooks, heard of his remarks. While Brooks would have dueled Sumner, he thought Sumner was less of an equal after his remarks and decided a beating was more humiliating and deserving.

Brooks decided to take matters into his own hands and attacked Sumner in the Senate chamber with his metal-tipped cane. After a minute of brutal beating, Sumner and Brooks were broken up, and Brooks walked out of the Senate chamber.

Because of the attack, both men became heroes in their respective regions. Brooks survived a vote to expel him from Congress, resigned to prove he had a large following back home, and was promptly voted back into Congress. Sumner's injuries kept him out of Congress for three years, but he continued to serve as a senator for several more years.

April 2

I WISH I WAS IN DIXIE!

Music has been called a universal language, as it can cross all language barriers and be understood by all. Music is also a great morale booster, and armies have used it for centuries. One of the most popular songs during the Civil War was the Confederate song *Dixie*.

However, this popular Confederate song *Dixie* was actually written by a northerner and loyal Unionist. Written in 1859 by Daniel Emmett, it had become a hit throughout the country by the start of the Civil War. Iy was adopted in the South because of its current popularity. According to some, the land of Dixie was in reference to a New Orleans bank that issued ten dollar notes with the French word *dix*, meaning "ten," on the front of the bill.

The song was a part of a minstrel show and was performed in blackface. However, what it represented was wrong, even though in the day it was considered acceptable. The Confederate leaders greatly enjoyed the song *Dixie* and even played it at Jefferson Davis's inauguration.

Remarkable Remark
"I have always thought 'Dixie' one of the best tunes I have ever heard. Our adversaries over the way attempted to appropriate it, but I insisted yesterday that we fairly captured it."
—Abe Lincoln

Exciting Entry
On this day in 1833, Union officer Thomas Howard Ruger was born. Ruger was Georgia's provisional governor in 1868 and oversaw the state government moving from Milledgeville to Atlanta.

Prominent Passing
On this day in 1865, CSA general A. P. Hill died. Hill was roommates with future Union general George McClellan while at West Point and would compete for a woman's heart, eventually McClellan's wife.

Lincoln enjoyed the tune after hearing it and asked for it to be played at the end of the Civil War. Lincoln believed that music, and especially *Dixie*, was a great way to help reunify the nation after a long war. While *Dixie* is no longer performed in minstrel shows, its popularity is still almost as strong today as it was during the Civil War.

April 3

THE KING AND I

Exciting Entry
On this day in 1842, Union officer Ulric Dahlgren was born. He was killed during a raid, carrying orders to kill Confederate President Jefferson Davis. However, Dahlgren's father believed they were forgeries.

Prominent Passing
On this day in 1867, Confederate secretary of war George Wythe Randolph died. He was the grandson of Thomas Jefferson, and as secretary of war, he wanted to retake New Orleans, but it never happened.

Most movies are based on books, and occasionally those books are rooted in historical events. One such historical lineup occurred in 1861, when King Mongkut of Siam wrote to the president of the United States and offered him elephants.

King Mongkut sent the president a sword, a photograph of himself and his daughter, two elephant tusks, and the offer to send the United States several elephants. While written to President Buchanan, it was Lincoln who eventually and respectfully declined the very generous offer, as the climate would not have been right and America had moved on toward steam power.

Lincoln turned over the gifts to the National Archives because of restrictions placed on receiving gifts in the Constitution. Many believe that the king offered the United States war elephants; however, he merely offered to send elephants to be released in America, not to be specifically used for war.

There is a scene in the 1956 movie *The King and I* in which this letter is being dictated, but to Lincoln, not Buchanan. Ironically, the movie that made Thailand a more famous country is banned in the country because it disrespects their royal family. While Lincoln declined the elephants, other animals like bears, dogs, camels, badgers, and an eagle were used in war or kept as mascots.

April 4

1ST UNITED STATES SHARPSHOOTERS

Modern-day American snipers can trace their roots back to the 1st United States Sharpshooters, an infantry regiment in the Union Army during the American Civil War. The original purpose of the sharpshooters was to eliminate high-ranking Confederate officers.

Hiram Berdan, one of the United States' leading marksmen, developed a plan to form a regiment of the country's top marksmen following the attack on Fort Sumter. To qualify for the regiment, volunteers had to hit a ten-inch target from two hundred yards away on ten consecutive shots.

The uniforms given to the marksmen were unique compared to the rest of the Union Army. Instead of the standard blue, those in the 1st United States Sharpshooters (and eventually the 2nd as well) were given green caps, coats, and trousers.

At the beginning of the war, the men used their own weapons, but this led to supply difficulties as the weapons were not all the same. Eventually, each soldier was given a Sharps rifle, issued by the Union government, after Berdan tried one that an old western miner and hunter had brought with him.

According to some, the 1st and 2nd Regiments were able to boast that they killed more Confederates than any other two regiments in the Union Army.

Remarkable Remark

"On each of our posts was stationed one of Berdan's sharp shooters, who were always on the look out for game, and woe to the rebel who put himself in their way."
—*Alfred Bellard*

Exciting Entry

On this day in 1817, Union general John Wilson Sprague was born. He earned the Medal of Honor posthumously for saving the Sherman's supply train from the Confederate force on their March to the Sea.

Prominent Passing

On this day in 1864, Union officer Joseph Pitty Couthouy died. Couthouy commanded several ships, including an ironclad vessel, during his service, and died after being ambushed and shot.

April 5

WOMEN IN THE CIVIL WAR

Exciting Entry
On this day in 1825, Confederate general David Rumph Jones was born. Jones was related to both Jefferson Davis and Zachary Taylor and saw action at the battles of Fort Sumter, Bull Run, and Antietam.

Prominent Passing
On this day in 1917, Union soldier Patrick Ginley died. He served in the Crimean War and American Civil War and earned the Medal of Honor for his bravery at the battle of Reams' Station in Virginia.

The Civil War saw thousands of men fighting; however, there were over four hundred women either openly or secretly serving in battle, and thousands more serving in non-combative roles.

In the North, roughly twenty thousand women worked as cooks, nurses, and laundresses. Women like Dorothea Dix and Louisa May Alcott were Union nurses during the war.

In the South, women worked as hard, providing food, clothing, and supplies for their soldiers even though they had fewer resources. Female slaves were left at their homes to continue supporting their masters' needs.

Women on both sides did whatever it took to fight, including hiding their identities. Maria "Belle" Boyd served as a Confederate spy and was an invaluable resource of information. She was arrested and released several times and eventually went to England where she wrote her memoirs. She died in poverty and was buried in Wisconsin.

Harriet Tubman was a conductor on the Underground Railroad, but she also served with the Union Army. She began her war efforts tending wounded, and in 1863, Tubman led a raid and rescued around seven hundred slaves, and became a bigger hero than before. For many of these women that served, their heroic actions are not forgotten.

INCOME TAX AND THE CIVIL WAR

While many think of the income tax as first starting with the passing of the Sixteenth Amendment, the income tax was first used during the Civil War.

In 1861, Lincoln and Congress authorized a 3% tax on yearly incomes over $800, which was a much-higher-than-average yearly income for most. However, in 1862, Abraham Lincoln signed another bill that imposed a 3% tax on incomes from $600 to $10,000 and a 5% tax on any income higher than $10,000.

The law was amended in 1864 to levy a tax of 5% on incomes between $600 and $5,000, 7.5% tax on incomes from $5,000 to $10,000 range, and a 10% tax on everything higher than $10,000.

The Confederacy also collected income taxes, approving its first national income tax measure, a graduated income tax, in 1863. It exempted wages up to $1,000 and levied a 1% tax on the next $1,500 of income. The Confederacy also placed a 2% tax on everything over $2,500. However, the Confederacy had no way to collect the revenue due it, and little of their revenue came from taxes. They revised the tax laws in 1864, but by that time it was too late.

The income tax was suspended by 1871, but the organization that was started in 1862 to collect the tax was never shut down. Today we call that organization the Internal Revenue Service.

Remarkable Remark

"There may be some irregularities…but if we should wait before collecting a tax to adjust the taxes upon each man in exact proportion with every other man, we should never collect any tax at all."
—*Abraham Lincoln*

Exciting Entry

On this day in 1828, Confederate general Charles W. Field was born. He served bravely in several key battles and was the House of Representatives doorkeeper for several years following the war.

Prominent Passing

On this day in 1862, Confederate general Albert Sidney Johnston died. He served as a general in three different countries' armies: the US Army, the Texas Army, and the Confederate Army.

April 7

LINCOLN'S ELECTION & INAUGURATION

Remarkable Remark

"God has honored you this day, in the sight of all the people. Will you honor Him in the White House?"

—*Secret Lincoln supporter*

Exciting Entry

On this day in 1801, Union Commodore Henry Eagle was born. Commodore Eagle was a brave officer, leading one of the Civil War's first naval attacks. He also participated in the Union blockade.

Prominent Passing

On this day in 1895, Confederate general James L. Kemper died. Kemper was wounded during Pickett's Charge and later captured. He practiced law and became Virginia's governor after the Civil War.

To many Americans, Abraham Lincoln's election and subsequent inauguration in 1861 brought uncertainty to their nation's future. Many wondered if Lincoln would resolve the nation's issues, or if his election would be the catalyst to greater problems.

Soon after Lincoln was elected, cities either rioted or paraded in the streets based on the prevailing sentiments of the town. In Springfield, Illinois, where Lincoln was during the election, supporters stayed up all night partying. Other supporters and well-wishers sent him telegrams of encouragement and support.

However, in the South, where Lincoln got few votes, many were upset. One telegram to Lincoln from an unknown citizen in Pensacola, Florida, stated, "You were last night hung in effigy in this city," and was signed, "a citizen." By the time Lincoln was sworn in, the states of South Carolina, Mississippi, Florida, Alabama, Georgia, Louisiana, and Texas had already ceded.

As Lincoln's inauguration approached, legislators tried to resolve the issue to no avail by compromise. In Lincoln's inaugural address, he let the nation know his goals of not interfering with the institution of slavery within the states but within federal territory. However, that pledge was not enough to stop the Civil War which followed.

April 8

POET TURNED UNION "NURSE"

During the Civil War, thousands of soldiers were wounded, and many men and women did their part to help the wounded. Popular poet Walt Whitman served as a nurse of sorts; but, he was more of a attentive visitor. The hospitals would even enforce visiting hours to keep him from constantly coming. While not an actual nurse, his visits helped boost morale in the hospitals.

He originally went to tend to his wounded brother George, but when he arrived, he found out his brother was fine. However, upon seeing the devastation, he began visiting the wounded and continued to visit them for three years. He visited the wounded and wrote letters, listened to their stories, and tended to their needs. He even brought ice cream for an entire hospital!

He was already considered a famous poet (*Leaves of Grass* first came out in 1855), yet he decided to help those who were wounded. According to Whitman, he visited up to 100,000 wounded and sick in his 600 visits and tours. His time visiting the wounded had a profound effect on his life, and several of his later poems reflected this effect.

Remarkable Remark
"I go around among these sights among the crowded hospitals doing what I can yet it is a mere drop in the bucket."
—*Walt Whitman*

Exciting Entry
On this day in 1828, Confederate officer George Baird Hodge was born. Hodge served in both the Confederate military and Confederate Congress during the war and was known for his bravery in battle.

Prominent Passing
On this day in 1899, Union officer John Wesley Turner died. After Turner retired from military duty, he moved to St. Louis and helped build the city infrastructure from dirt roads to well-paved ones.

Whitman wrote several poems as a result of his three years of work and published them in his book *Drum Taps*, which included "When Lilacs Last in the Dooryard Bloom'd" and "O Captain! My Captain!"

SIOUX UPRISING

Remarkable Remark
"We are in the midst of a most terrible and exciting Indian war... A wild panic prevails in nearly one-half of the state."
—*Telegraph sent to Lincoln*

Exciting Entry
On this day in 1826, Union officer Thomas Hewson Neill was born. He was a career soldier that fought at Richmond, Gettysburg, and many other battles and was commended for his repeated bravery.

Prominent Passing
On this day in 1898, Confederate officer James Ronald Chalmers died. After the War ended, Chalmers became a Congressman from Mississippi after the state was readmitted into the United States.

In 1862, the continuing problems in the Dakota Territory between settlers broke out into fighting. This Sioux Uprising, caused by late government payments, forced relocation, and a poor harvest, led to hundreds brutally killed and thousands more displaced from their homes.

The uprising began when a few starving braves tried to steal chicken eggs and called one in their party a coward. In an attempt to prove that none of them were cowards, they decided to shoot the chickens' owner and his family and friends. Scared of retaliation by the settlers and the government, the Dakota Indians decided to attack first.

The scared settlers tried to send their wives and children to safety while they defended their towns. The defenders eventually grew to several hundred well-armed volunteers and US Army soldiers, and over the next few weeks defeated the Indians in several battles. After General John Pope lost the Second Battle of Bull Run, Lincoln decided to send him to command the fighting against the Dakota Indians and oversee the war.

After battles at Birch Coulee and Wood Lake, the Sioux Uprising was considered virtually ended. Over three hundred Dakota were sentenced to death, but Lincoln commuted all but thirty-eight of the men's sentences. On December 26, 1862, all thirty-eight men were hanged in America's largest mass execution in its history.

A DESERTER, I PRESUME?

Famed explorer and journalist Henry Stanley, the same person who looked for missionary doctor David Livingston, served in the Civil War. But not only did he serve in the Civil War, he also served on both sides.

Henry Stanley, whose real name was John Rowlands, never wanted to fight and was labeled a coward in his town. Stanley started on the Confederate side as a private in the Dixie Grays. After being captured at Shiloh, Stanley was sent to Camp Douglas, a POW camp outside of Chicago. Six weeks later, he was given and took the opportunity to swear allegiance to the North and fight in their army.

However, Stanley was hospitalized with dysentery; when he recovered, he deserted instead of rejoining. He headed back home to England, but his mother told him not to come back until he made something of himself. Stanley returned to New York, where he joined the Union Navy as a ship's clerk onboard the USS *Minnesota*. It was during this time that he began to write more frequently and even had several detailed accounts of battles printed.

Remarkable Remark
"It was...the first time that Glory sickened me with its repulsive aspect, and made me suspect it was all a glittering lie."
—*Henry Stanley*

Exciting Entry
On this day in 1806, Confederate general Leonidas Polk was born. Polk was a soldier turned preacher turned soldier. Polk was a beloved officer but died when a cannonball ripped through his body.

Prominent Passing
On this day in 1862, Union officer William Harvey Lamb Wallace died. Wallace served bravely in several battles and was mortally wounded at the Battle of Shiloh when shrapnel hit him in the head.

However, Stanley again deserted and eventually made his career in journalism. He is possibly the only man to have deserted both the Confederate and Union armies and the Union navy.

EARLY EMANCIPATION ATTEMPTS

Exciting Entry

On this day in 1837, Union officer Elmer Ephraim Ellsworth was born. He was a good friend of Lincoln's and is considered the first Union officer killed in the war after lowering a Confederate flag.

Prominent Passing

On this day in 1900, Confederate general Seth Barton died. After the war, Barton began studying chemistry purely as a hobby and was soon considered one of the leading chemists of his day.

While many remember the Emancipation Proclamation as the beginning of the end to slavery, there were several attempts by Union members to free slaves even before the Proclamation.

In 1861, several slaves that were forced to work on Southern fortifications fled to the Union side, where Union general Benjamin Butler declared the men to be "contraband of war" and not fugitive slaves. By the end of the war, thousands of slaves were classified as contraband and put in camps, but they were still not freedmen.

In 1861, General John Fremont declared the Department of Missouri, the area under his control, to be under martial law, and for all slaves to be free. However, Lincoln announced that Fremont's order went against a congressional law, and that slaves in Missouri were still not free.

In 1862, General David Hunter declared that slaves in his Department of the South were free. However, Lincoln once again revoked the order since he believed it was the president's role to free the slaves.

In 1862, Congress passed laws abolishing slavery in Washington D.C. and federal territories, declaring contraband slaves free, and allowing black men to serve in the military. Lincoln would issue a Preliminary Emancipation Proclamation in September 1862, and it went into effect on January 1, 1863, officially making the war about freeing the slaves.

CHILDREN IN THE CIVIL WAR

The Civil War affected not just men and women, but also children. Boys ranging from eight to eighteen would serve in the military, often lying about their age; while those staying home, especially in the South, experienced the results of battle firsthand.

Boys like Johnny Clem (age 9), Edwin Jemison (age 16), and John Cook (age 14) were under the legal fighting age, but they willingly signed up to fight for their respective sides. In 1862, Susie Taylor (age 14) became the first black teacher to openly teach other African Americans.

Children at home also saw the horrors of war. In the South, the war front was often the little children's town. Many of these children saw bloodshed and battles firsthand, even though they weren't fighting.

In the North, although there were fewer major battles, children still felt the effect of war. Many young children saw fighting happen just down the street from them during the Battle of Gettysburg.

At school, children were taught how to be patriotic, and they pretended to be soldiers or nurses. However, simple things like birthday cake and presents were no longer easy to come by, and some parents even told their children that Santa Claus had been killed. Children experienced the Civil War, and they became the hope for a greater future of America.

Remarkable Remark

"One of the pathetic sights that I remember was a poor Confederate…[and] At the sight of the poor boy's corpse, I burst into a regular boo-hoo, and started on."
—*John Cockerill (age 16)*

Exciting Entry

On this day in 1831, Union officer Grenville M. Dodge was born. He was the chief engineer for the Union Pacific Railroad and helped build the transcontinental railroad and several other railroads.

Prominent Passing

On this day in 1864, Confederate general Thomas Green died. Green was considered one of the South's best officers and participated in several battles in Texas and the New Mexico Territory.

 *April* **13**

GENERAL ULYSSES GRANT AND THE JEWS

In 1861, Grant took the town of Paducah, Kentucky, where many Jewish merchants resided. The Union ordered all merchants to have a permit to continue trading. However, smuggling began and declined the shaky mutual trust between the Union and the secessionists and Jews.

However, when Grant's father, along with several Jewish merchants, tried to use his son's position for gain, Grant hastily issued General Order No. 11, expelling all Jews from the area under his control. One Jew named Cesar Kaskel was ordered to leave pursuant General Order No. 11 in twenty-four hours.

Lincoln, who was to issue the Emancipation Proclamation in a few days, never saw the order, but Kaskel wrote a letter about the deed to the press, and the papers published it. Kaskel traveled to Washington, gaining the support of many he talked to, and set up a meeting between Lincoln and himself. Lincoln condemned and revoked Grant's order.

Both houses of Congress proposed resolutions to condemn Grant's General Order No. 11. While neither resolution was passed, national coverage in the newspapers lasted about another week. This order did not greatly affect Grant as he went on to become president. Grant did apologize for the order and became one of the Jews' greatest supporters, naming more Jews to government offices than any previous president.

EMANCIPATION PROCLAMATION

Regarded by Lincoln as his greatest achievement, the Emancipation Proclamation, or Proclamation 95, could essentially do nothing until the war ended.

Lincoln had written an early draft of the Proclamation in 1862; however, he did not want to enforce it until the Union had a major victory. The Battle of Antietam was the victory Lincoln needed, and he issued the Emancipation Proclamation on January 1, 1863.

The Proclamation left all slaves in the Border States, the North, and in places under Union control in the same position as prior to the war. It did free slaves from the states in rebellion; however, it could not be enforced until the Union captured the areas still under Confederate control.

One immediate thing his Proclamation did was keep Europe out of the war. The South was lobbying for European help, and many foreign nations were close to helping. However, when Lincoln declared that the new reason for fighting was to free slaves, Europe would not help the South because Europe themselves had passed laws to free their slaves and were opposed to the practice.

Remarkable Remark
"I can only trust in God, I have made no mistake.... It is now for the country and the world to pass judgment on it [Emancipation Proclamation]."
—*Abraham Lincoln*

Exciting Entry
On this day in 1820, Confederate general Harry T. Hays was born. He served valiantly in several battles, and once when captured he fled on horseback through heavy fire until he safely got away.

Prominent Passing
On this day in 1909, Confederate officer Matthew C. Butler died. After the war, Butler served in the US Senate and as a major general of volunteers in the US Army during the Spanish-American War.

However, the slaves would not truly be free until the Thirteenth Amendment. Congress and the states quickly ratified the Thirteenth Amendment, granting slaves their freedom. Sadly, Jim Crow laws quickly enveloped the South, giving the African American freedom without true freedom.

STUBBORN MINNESOTA

Remarkable Remark
"The flag's story clearly transcends state boundaries. Legally and ethically, the bond between this flag and the people of Minnesota should not be taken lightly."
—Nina Archibald

Exciting Entry
On this day in 1820, Confederate officer Evander McNair was born. McNair served valiantly in the Western Theater and Trans-Mississippi Theater and was considered a decent Christian leader.

Prominent Passing
On this day in 1865, President Abraham Lincoln died. While known for being the president during the Civil War, Lincoln is also the only president to hold a patent for an invention relating to boats.

At the Battle of Gettysburg in 1863, Private Marshall Sherman of the First Minnesota Volunteer Infantry Regiment, Company C, captured the battle flag of the Twenty-Eighth Virginia Volunteer Infantry Regiment during Pickett's Charge. Sherman later received a Medal of Honor for his role in the Battle of Gettysburg.

After the battle, the Virginian flag was turned over to the War Department, where it was somehow returned back to Minnesota by 1888. However, when Congress and the president ordered all Civil War possessions to be returned in a spirit of reconciliation, Minnesota never returned the Virginia flag because the order only pertained to flags owned by the War Department.

What makes this event interesting is that Minnesota refuses to return the flag even though Virginia has requested for it to be returned. Virginia legislation has repeatedly given approval for its return, but each time, Minnesota refuses stating they earned the right to the flag in battle.

Virginia requested or had the flag's return requested in 1961, 1998, 2000, 2002, 2003, 2011, and 2015, but Minnesota resolutely denied the requests. Ironically, Minnesota returned one of its captured Georgia flags, and then reminded Virginia that it still held their flag. The flag is currently held by the Minnesota State Historical Society.

April 16

BITTER VICKSBURG

As the war in the West continued, the Union continued its war effort to control the Mississippi River. General Ulysses Grant began his offensive against Vicksburg in May of 1863 and would end it over a month later on July 4, 1863, Independence Day.

Although Grant forced the Confederate Army into Vicksburg, direct assaults against the city were repelled, and Grant decided to siege the city. Vicksburg was built on high bluffs and large swamps to the North and could easily defend itself from Union attacks. However, Grant was determined to take the city; and once he had the Confederates trapped, he built fifteen miles of trenches around the city and waited the Confederates out.

Many tried to escape Vicksburg, but the retreating Confederates made escaping impossible and many citizens were stuck inside the city during the forty-seven-day siege. The lack of food and resources prevented the city's residents from living a normal life. Confederate leaders recommended moving to caves for protection from the constant Union shelling.

Remarkable Remark

"A Parrott shell...fell in the centre of the cave before us all...Our fate seemed almost certain....when George, the servant boy...seized the shell, and threw it into the street."
—*Mary Ann Loughborough*

Exciting Entry

On this day in 1816, Confederate general Edward "Alleghany" Johnson was born. Johnson was a brave leader and took over "Stonewall" Jackson's division after Jackson died from friendly fire.

Prominent Passing

On this day in 1865, Confederate officer Robert C. Tyler died. He lost a leg in battle and was killed by Union sharpshooters. He is considered the last Confederate general to be killed in battle.

Citizens and soldiers eventually surrendered to Union forces after suffering dehydration and malnutrition. However, the harshness of the siege left a bitter taste with Vicksburg's residents, and they did not officially celebrate July 4 until after WWII, eighty-one years later.

A CASE OF MISTAKEN IDENTITY

April 17

Remarkable Remark
"When the troops that effected our capture came up…you know how deeply we were disappointed in their identity."
—Abel Comstock

Exciting Entry
On this day in 1813, Union general Henry Washington Benham was born. Benham fought in every major battle that the Army of the Potomac fought in, from Chancellorsville to Lee's surrender.

Prominent Passing
On this day in 1863, Confederate general Daniel Smith Donelson died. Several days after his death, the Confederate Congress promoted him, not knowing that he had died.

Often, mistaken identity can lead to problems, and mistaken identitiy in the Civil War was no exception.

There was a Union General named "Jefferson Davis" who had the misfortune of sharing the same name as the Confederate President. The Union "Jeff Davis" was notorious for having killed his superior officer and getting away with it.

Surprisingly, this name confusion only caused problems one time for the Union. In 1863, during the Battle of Chickamauga, near Horseshoe Ridge, as the evening began to come, skirmishes between the two armies continued but slowly began to wind down.

However, the Union's 21st Ohio regiment of volunteers noticed a large group of men advancing toward them. While most assumed they were Union reinforcements, a few were wary and one soldier called out seeking identification. The returning reply was "Jeff Davis' troops." The Union troops feeling safer, now that they knew the men were Union soldiers, were shocked when guns were suddenly pointed at them, and they were ordered to surrender by the 7th Regiment Florida infantry. Many Union soldiers were able to escape as a skirmish among the advancing Confederate troops broke out in the dark.

It was simply a case of mistaken identity, but it caused a portion of the Union's 21st Ohio regiment to surrender to the Confederate army.

April **18**

US BALLOON CORPS

During the Civil War, a major part of each battle was reconnaissance and troop movements. One way each side did this was by using balloons.

These balloons were used in Washington D.C. and Manassas in 1861 and the 1862 Peninsula Campaign, and they were employed during the Fredericksburg (1862) and Chancellorsville (1863) campaigns.

In the West, balloons were used to support the campaign against Island Number 10 in the Mississippi River, while Confederate balloons were employed around Richmond during the Seven Days Campaign.

Most balloons carried one to five people depending on its size, and most balloons were designed to just be tethered into the ground while staying roughly one thousand feet above the ground. Even though these balloons were often very colorful, none were ever shot down because of how high they were.

The US Balloon Corps would often hover over Union ships and report battle movements. However, some reports were vague and therefore of little help to the commanding officer. The observations made from the balloon were transmitted either by telegraph or signal flags, and their use was considered valuable by many generals and even Lincoln. The Union Army decided to terminate its balloon corps in 1863, despite it being well received.

Remarkable Remark
"I have never understood why the enemy abandoned the use of military balloons early in 1863, after having used them extensively up to that time."
—*E. P. Alexander*

Exciting Entry
On this day in 1813, Dr. James McCune Smith was born. Dr. Smith was the first African American to hold a medical degree and lived long enough to see the Civil War end and slaves go free.

Prominent Passing
On this day in 1924, Union officer Horatio Gates Gibson died. Gibson was honored for his valiant service by being allowed to give the commencement address to the West Point graduates twice.

April **19**

BRUSHFIRE IN THE WILDERNESS

Exciting Entry

On this day in 1821, Union officer Mortimer Dormer Leggett was born. During the Atlanta Campaign, Leggett captured a hill and was honored for his actions by having the hill renamed Leggett's Hill.

Prominent Passing

On this day in 1900, Union officer Henry Demas died. Demas was born a slave but joined and served in a Union colored regiment. After the Civil War, he became a well-known, local politician.

The Battle of the Wilderness was the opening battle of the 1864 Overland Campaign. Roughly 101,000 Union soldiers fought nearly 61,000 Confederate troops, and the ensuing battle left over 29,000 casualties. However, of the thousands of men that died, several hundred died from a brushfire.

The Wilderness was an area of thick shrubs and dense forests. One soldier recounted that the visibility within the area was only about one hundred yards. On the night of May 6, 1864, as men continued fighting, the rifles' bursts caused multiple brushfires to break out in between the two armies.

While attempts to save fellow comrades occurred during the evening, the heroic effort was not enough to save all the wounded that day. The men in the camps could hear their wounded comrades screaming while they were being burned alive throughout the night.

Up to eight hundred men died in this horrific way. The Battle of the Wilderness saw almost 30,000 casualties and was one of the first times the Union did not retreat after a bloody battle. Although the battle was a draw, many of the Union men cheered as they heard the news that they would continue the advance.

April **20**

UNION PRISONER OF WAR CAMP

While many remember the Southern prisoner of war camps, many forget that the Union also had them. From July 6, 1864 until July 11, 1865, Union prison camp Elmira in New York incarcerated a total of 12,123 Confederates.

This camp was nicknamed "Hellmira" because of the fact that the terrible conditions led the camp to have a 25% mortality rate. Comparably, Andersonville had roughly a 27% mortality rate. However, Andersonville also had nearly six times the number of soldiers die in their camp.

On top of that, the Union built observation towers and charged around fifteen cents for a person to view the prisoners and even sold refreshments. Many of the prisoners would do cartwheels, juggle, and do other tricks when people began to watch. However, Union soldiers put an end to the performing and made the prisoners just stand there.

Conditions were made worse because of the fact that the camp could house up to 5,000 prisoners, meaning that the other 7,000 prisoners had to live in tents along a nearby river. During the cold winter months, this river would also flood and cause dozens of deaths.

Neither side was ready for a long war, and many POW camps were understaffed and underprepared, resulting in high mortality rates. It was just another sad reality of a long, hard war.

Remarkable Remark

"The treatment I received was as good as could be expected. The barracks were not very comfortable. The food was common, but I lived on it."

—J. L. Camp

Exciting Entry

On this day in 1824, Confederate officer Alfred Holt Colquitt was born. Colquitt served heroically during the Civil War and after the war served as Georgia's governor and later as its US Senator.

Prominent Passing

On this day in 1910, Confederate officer Samuel Gibbs French died. French served heroically under several men and eventually moved to Florida to be a planter. He is buried in Pensacola, Florida.

April **21**

LINCOLN'S REPRESENTATIVE RECRUIT

During the Civil War, men were allowed to hire a substitute in the military. However, most people do not realize that Abraham Lincoln hired a substitute even though he was exempt because of his age and the fact that he was the president.

On October 1, 1864, Lincoln hired John Summerfield Staples as a representative recruit for him in the military. His enlistment form had crossed out "substitute" and replaced it with "representative," as Lincoln wanted to promote his new military enlistment program.

Lincoln wanted older men and exempt men to hire a substitute for the army, and to encourage others, he hired a representative recruit. Staples had previously substituted for another man but was discharged in 1863 because he was too ill to continue fighting.

In 1864, he moved to DC and was approached and asked if he would serve for the president. Staples met with Lincoln at the White House, and Lincoln offered him $500 for his services. Staples saw little action as Lincoln's representative recruit.

After the war, he applied for a pension but was denied. He had very little recognition until he died in 1888. A bridge was named after him, but a flood washed the bridge and plaque away. Later historic markers indicating his service were placed after the flood.

NORTHERNMOST CONFEDERATE LAND ACTION

While Gettysburg is considered the farthest north the Confederacy attacked in a major engagement, there were several minor skirmishes, raids, and fights even farther north. The northernmost Confederate land action occurred in St. Albans, Vermont, on October 19, 1864.

The raid was authorized by the Confederate government, and Confederate Lieutenant Bennett Young was the leader of the St. Albans Raid. Young's men were escaped Confederate prisoners that had fled to Canada. A group of eighteen to twenty-two men traveled into town by train over ten days, and then began to blend in with the town's citizens.

At 3 p.m. on October 19, Young announced to the gathering people near his hotel that the Confederate States of America now controlled the town. His men split up and robbed three banks. While taking some townspeople hostage, he made them swear loyalty to the South.

The men stole over $200,000, killed a man, and then fled the town. Within twenty-four hours, most of the men were captured and turned over to Canadian authorities, although none were convicted. Young continued to taunt the townspeople of St. Albans by sending money to pay for his hotel room and writing a letter asking for copies of the town's newspaper. Young was pardoned in 1868 and ran a successful law practice until his death in 1919.

Remarkable Remark

"Gentlemen, I am an officer of the Confederate army. I've been sent here to take this town [St. Albans], and I'm gonna do it."
— *Bennett Young*

Exciting Entry

On this day in 1818, Union officer Cadwallader Washburn was born. He served bravely during the war, and after the war ended, he started Washburn, Crosby & Company, the forerunner of General Mills.

Prominent Passing

On this day in 1865, Union naval officer William McKean died. McKean commanded the East Gulf Blockading Squadron and directed attacks on several areas, including the Pensacola Navy Yard.

SURRENDER AT APPOMATTOX COURT HOUSE

Exciting Entry

On this day in 1791, President James Buchanan was born. He was considered a poor president for not stopping Southern states from ceding and published a memoir attempting to vindicate his presidency.

Prominent Passing

On this day in 1865, Confederate officer James Dearing died. During the Confederate retreat to Appomattox Court House, he was fatally wounded by a Union officer that he later killed in a pistol duel.

On April 9, 1865, Robert E. Lee surrendered the 28,000-man Army of Northern Virginia to Ulysses S. Grant at Appomattox Court House.

While most associate this event with the end of the American Civil War, General Johnston surrendered his army and numerous smaller garrisons to Maj. Gen. William T. Sherman on April 26. Johnston's surrender was the largest of the war, totaling almost 90,000 men.

The final battle of the Civil War took place at Palmita Ranch in Texas on May 11–12. The last large Confederate military force was surrendered on June 2 by Gen. Edmund Kirby Smith in Galveston, Texas, and the CSS *Shenandoah* did not surrender until November 1865. By this time, the broken country had begun to pick up the pieces from years of fighting and headed into the Reconstruction period.

The final draft of the surrender document was written by Ely S. Parker, a Native American from the Seneca tribe. He held the rank of lieutenant colonel during the war, serving as Ulysses S. Grant's adjutant and secretary. When Lee commented on Parker's prominent position, Parker reminded Lee and the others that they were all still Americans. When Grant won the presidency, Parker was the first Native American to be appointed as Commissioner of Indian Affairs.

THE MANY ATTEMPTS ON LINCOLN'S LIFE

When you think of Abraham Lincoln, you probably think about his Emancipation Proclamation or his assassination. But did you know that John Wilkes Booth's successful murder was not the first attempt on Lincoln's life?

In 1861, president-elect Lincoln was on his way to be inaugurated. However, his personal secretary that handled his mail became worried over the amount of hate mail Lincoln was receiving and received word of a possible attempt to take over the railroad in Baltimore.

Additionally, the president of the railroad that Lincoln was using had heard rumors of possible destruction or murder and contacted Allan Pinkerton. Pinkerton was brought in as logistical security for the railroad and soon uncovered an attempt on Lincoln's life. Receiving the information, Lincoln avoided the assassination attempt and arrived safely in Washington D.C.

About nine months before Lincoln was assassinated, he was heading home at night when suddenly a shot was heard from about fifty yards out that startled the horse. Lincoln quickly rode home and a guard noticed he was missing his hat. Lincoln joked that it was probably just a hunter and an accident. However, when the hat was retrieved, they found a bullet hole in the hat. An assassin was eventually successful and Lincoln died on April 15, 1865. His plans to bind the nation's wounds were cut short, yet his legacy continues to this day.

Remarkable Remark
"Every night as I mingled among them I could hear the most outrageous sentiments enunciated. No man's life was safe in the hands of those men."
—Allan Pinkerton

Exciting Entry
On this day in 1807, Union officer Charles Ferguson Smith was born. He served in several battles under Ulysses Grant, who was previously his student at West Point and admired Smith's leadership.

Prominent Passing
On this day in 1904, Union soldier William Pittenger died. He was one of the first men in the Civil War to receive the Medal of Honor for his bravery in a raid nicknamed the "Great Locomotive Chase."

April 25

CHRISTIANITY IN THE CIVIL WAR

Exciting Entry

On this day in 1840, Confederate officer James Dearing was born. He was mortally wounded (April 23) and is considered to be the last Confederate general to die as a result of a battle wound.

Prominent Passing

On this day in 1862, Union officer Charles F. Smith died. Smith wounded his leg after jumping aboard a boat. He died after the wound became infected.

During the Civil War, Christianity played an important part of the soldier's everyday life. Christianity affected soldiers, citizens, and freedmen, and its results carried on long after the war.

Many societies provided Christian materials. In 1864, the American Bible Society distributed over 900,000 copies of the Bible. The Christian Commission handed out over 500,000 copies of the Bible in the Union and several million copies in the Confederacy.

In the North, General McClellan made sure his soldiers attended church regularly, and General Rosecrans tried to never fight on a Sunday. General Howard could often be seen preaching to his troops. Freedmen built wealthy, Christian settlements during and after the war to promote the gospel.

In the South, General Lee promoted observing the Sabbath among his men. General Jackson distributed gospel tracts and often prayed for his men.

During the war, revival broke out among both armies. Confederate soldiers eagerly sought Bibles and could be heard singing during their retreat towards Atlanta. In the north, hundreds of soldiers had to be turned away from the overcrowded brigade chapels. Roughly 300,000 soldiers, or 10% of all the men engaged, from both sides were saved.

THE FINAL CONFEDERATES TO SURRENDER

While most think of Lee's surrender at Appomattox Court House as the end of the Civil War, the final group of Confederates to surrender was not until November 5, 1865.

The Confederate flag was surrendered after the CSS *Shenandoah* discovered that the Civil War was over. However, it was in England, not America, that they surrendered. They discovered the news from a British vessel and realized that they could be considered pirates now that the Confederacy no longer existed.

The captain stowed all weapons below deck and even repainted the hull. He fled halfway across the globe to Liverpool, England, the same place the Confederacy secretly purchased the vessel in 1864. The CSS *Shenandoah* had recorded capturing or destroying 38 ships, seizing more than 1,000 captives, and inflicting $1.6 million in damages. It did most of its damage in the Pacific Ocean against Union whaling ships. Some historians debate if the ship's captain knew the war was over and continued attacking ships, but no conclusive evidence has yet been uncovered.

Remarkable Remark

"Having received.... the sad intelligence of the overthrow of the Confederate government, all attempts to destroy shipping or property of the United States will cease from this date."
—CSS Shenandoah *log*

Exciting Entry

On this day in 1826, Confederate officer Ambrose R. Wright was born. At the Battle of Antietam, Wright was wounded twice but stayed in the battle and spent the next seven months healing.

Prominent Passing

On this day in 1865, John Wilkes Booth died. Booth originally wanted to kidnap President Lincoln; however, when that plan fell through, Booth decided to assassinate Lincoln instead.

After surrendering to the British, the sailors were eventually released, and the ship was returned to the US government. The ship was later sold to the sultan of Zanzibar and sank in 1872.

CIVIL WAR DEATHS

Exciting Entry

On this day in 1835, Union officer John Murray Corse was born. Corse was a brave soldier who would courageously lead a division of troops during General Sherman's famous March to the Sea.

Prominent Passing

On this day in 1893, Union officer John Murray Corse died. After the Civil War, he served as Boston's postmaster, and when he died, he was buried in Iowa, where he lived before the Civil War.

During the Civil War, over three million men fought. Of the soldiers who fought, roughly 620,000 of them died, and roughly two thirds died from disease. However, the total number of deaths has never been a set number, and it has once again been challenged by a history professor from New York.

Historically, the Civil War dead was determined to be 360,222 Union soldiers and 258,000 Confederate soldiers or roughly 620,000 total deaths. The South's numbers, however, were incomplete and faulty during the war and left the scholars to almost guestimate the number of deaths.

In 2011, historian J. David Hacker determined that the Civil War deaths actually number around 650,000–850,000 with an average of 750,000 dead. Instead of using military records, Hacker used the 1850–1860 and 1870–1880 census data and compared the ratio of male survival in relation to female survival in ten to fourty-four-year-old Americans.

He then took the 1860–1870 data and compared it to the average of the other two sets of data. This allowed him to determine how many more men died during the Civil War than was expected. This new data now suggests that an extra 20% died. However, some historians doubt the veracity of the data as there are still too many variables involved. The true numbers numbers may never be known.

FUTURE US LEADERS IN THE CIVIL WAR

Often times those great leaders in war become elevated to a position where they can run for a high office later in life. The Civil War was no exception, as several great leaders came from the war.

There were seven men who served during the Civil War that would later serve as the president of the United States. Ulysses Grant, Rutherford Hayes, James Garfield, Chester Arthur, Benjamin Harrison, and Andrew Johnson were all generals of different rank. William McKinley served as a Brevet Major during the war.

There was also at least seven future Supreme Court justices who served in the Civil War, with four serving on the Union side and the other three on the Confederate side. Another future justice hired a substitute during the war. Two of these future justices became prisoners of war. Possibly the most famous Supreme Court justice that served was Oliver Wendell Holmes Jr. Another official was President Buchanan's vice president, John Breckinridge, who after leaving office, served for the South.

Remarkable Remark

"We shall never know why slavery dies so hard in this Republic and in this Hall [Congress] till we know why sin outlives disaster, and Satan is immortal."
—James A. Garfield

Exciting Entry

On this day in 1812, Union general Daniel Henry Rucker was born. Rucker served as a quartermaster during the Civil War and was the father-in-law to Union general Philip Sheridan.

Prominent Passing

On this day in 1905, Confederate officer Fitzhugh Lee died. Lee was General Robert Lee's nephew and served bravely in the Civil War. After surrendering, he promoted peace within the Union.

Many people in government served in the Civil War, and it is certainly not limited to this group, as many people would go on to serve in important offices in their local and state positions. Many more would become congressmen in the years following the war, using their heroic deeds to help elevate them to a public office.

ARLINGTON NATIONAL CEMETERY

Remarkable Remark

"I recommend that… the land surrounding the Arlington Mansion, now understood to be the property of the United States, be appropriated as a National Military Cemetery."

-Montgomery Meigs

Exciting Entry

On this day in 1815, Union officer Abram Duryée was born. Prior to the Civil War, he made a large fortune importing mahogany. He became New York City's police commissioner after the war.

Prominent Passing

On this day in 1891, Confederate officer Armistead Lindsay Long died. He served as General Lee's military secretary for nearly two years and became an indispensable assistant to Lee.

General Robert Lee's Arlington was an estate that his wife had inherited from her father George Washington Parke Custis upon his death in 1857. However, by the end of the war, it had become a cemetery.

After Virginia seceded, the federal government took over Arlington so that the Confederate Army could not use the estate's strategic location to attack Washington D.C. As slaves became free, the Union Army used the land for a Freedmen's Village, and after the war, some of the freedmen remained and continued to farm parcels of land.

The property was sold to the government under circumstances later determined to be unconstitutional. As the war lingered, Union officials sought a place to bury the growing number of dead soldiers. Arlington was chosen and became a national military cemetery in 1864. Many men were interred on the grounds, but the question of Arlington's ownership was still unresolved when General Lee died.

Lee's son took the matter all the way to the Supreme Court which awarded Arlington back to the Lee family. However, they agreed to sell the property back to the government for $150,000, and the government accepted. Today, thousands visit the cemetery that honors the brave men and women who served the United States.

HORSE STATUE MYTH

If you ever went to a memorial or a battle site, you probably have seen a statue of a horse and rider. A guide may have also told you that the number of legs the horse has in the air tells how that person died. However, this is a myth.

The myth was started at the Gettysburg battle site between 1917–1932 by a few guides. At Gettysburg all the equestrian statues except one follow the hoof code that states "if the horse has two legs in the air, the rider died in battle; one leg in the air, the rider was hurt in battle and may have died later; and zero legs in the air, the rider was not wounded or killed in that battle and died by any other reason."

Tour guides at Gettysburg made up this code to help tourists learn about the military leaders that these statues represented. At Gettysburg, seven of the eight equestrian statues follow this legend, making it one of the closest battle sites that lines up with the myth, but General John Sedgwick's horse has all four hooves on the ground, even though he died in a battle.

Remarkable Remark
"The story that the posture of the horse in equestrian statues... seems to be one of those myths which grow up around historical places and are almost impossible to destroy."
-E. E. Davis

Exciting Entry
On this day in 1805, William Kerley Strong was born. He was a retired merchant traveling in Egypt when the Civil War started and swiftly went to France to buy weapons for the Union cause.

Prominent Passing
On this day in 1895, Union officer Davis Tillson died. After the war, Tillson was director of the Freedmen's Bureau in Georgia and then became a successful businessman in Maine.

Many historians refute this as myth, and Gettysburg's superintenent refuted the myth in the 1930s. The best way to visually prove this myth false is to view the equestrian statues at Washington D.C., where only about one third of all the statues follow these guidelines. Multiple equestrian statues of the same person tend to be inconsistent in terms of the horse's legs positioning.

May

PRESIDENTS

In the 230 plus years that the United States of America has existed, forty-five men have held the office of President of the United States of America. Many, like Washington and Lincoln, have been exalted to a legendary status; while others, like Pierce and Arthur, have all but been forgotten. These forty-five men have had their mix of good and bad, yet, every single one of them took the same oath to uphold the US Constitution and to lead the United States of America. These men have been considered some of the most powerful men in the world, and in the years to come, even more men and women may hold this exalted position.

However, there have been other kinds of presidents. Eight men were president of the United States under the Articles of Confederation. As industries expanded and companies were created, men were placed in the position of president. Sports teams, car companies, railroads, financial institutions, and more were all led by people with the title of president. As more countries aimed for freedom, many began having people titled as president to lead their countries. We hope that this May, you will learn many new presidents and discover more of what they accomplished.

May **1**

JOHN HANSON, AMERICA'S FIRST PRESIDENT?

Exciting Entry
On this day in 1898, Eugene R. Black was born. He was president of the World Bank and lent billions to help rebuild postwar Europe. He also grew the bank from forty-eight member nations to eighty nations.

Prominent Passing
On this day in 2008, Sir Anthony Mamo died. He was Malta's first elected president and held the office during the 1970s. His country respected him, as he was considered humble and a leader of integrity.

To many, George Washington is the United States' first president. However, Washington was the first president under the Constitution. John Hanson was the first president to serve a full term under the Articles of Confederation.

Each president (officially "President of the United States in Congress assembled") was supposed to serve a one year term. Hanson became the first full-term president under the Articles of Confederation in November of 1781.

Because the Articles did not set up an executive branch, the president's position was more ceremonial. Hanson was required to sign documents and handle communication, and he saw his duties as very tedious. Although he wanted to resign, his colleagues convinced him to stay by appealing to his sense of duty. Some historians state that Hanson helped start several government departments, remove foreign armies off American soil, and establish Thanksgiving.

However, in all reality, Hanson was merely responsible for signing any document approved by the Confederation Congress, including those establishing departments and official holidays. Also, the name "president" at that time was a recognized name for an official who merely presides or moderates. Though John Hanson was the first president under the Confederation Congress, he really wasn't America's first president.

WASHINGTON'S FINAL RESTING PLACE

Perhaps the best-known American president and easily one of the best-known Americans is George Washington. He served as Commander-in-Chief of the Continental Army and then served two terms as the first president under the Constitution.

When Washington died, he was immortalized by his friends and family, and Congress passed a resolution seeking the permission to place George Washington under a marble monument in the Capitol.

However, Washington requested in his will that he be buried at his home estate, Mount Vernon. When Martha Washington received Congress's request to bury her deceased husband in the Capitol, she agreed because she viewed it as the public's wish to honor her husband.

However, Congress spent several years debating over the cost and location of the memorial. The issue was brought up several times, including in 1824 by congressman and future president James Buchanan. In 1829, architects decided to place Washington's crypt (underground burial place) below the Capitol Rotunda.

Remarkable Remark
"[Washington] has been sleeping with his fathers for almost a quarter of a century, and his mortal remains have yet been unhonored by that people, who, with justice, call him the father of their country."
—*James Buchanan*

Exciting Entry
On this day in 1740, Elias Boudinot was born. He was the second president under the Articles of Confederation and was close friends with George Washington, Alexander Hamilton, and Robert Morris.

Prominent Passing
On this day in 2005, Wee Kim Wee died. He came from humble beginnings, but his hard work paid off when he became a diplomat for Singapore and eventually the first elected president of the country.

As the 1832 centennial celebration of Washington's birth approached, Congress once again asked Washington's family if they could move his body, but the family refused, and the matter was dropped. Washington's remains rest in Mount Vernon, and people can visit the crypt's location under the Capitol Rotunda.

JOHN ADAMS'S WHITE HOUSE

Remarkable Remark

"Before I end my Letter I pray Heaven to bestow the best of Blessings on this House and all that shall hereafter in habit it. May none but honest and wise Men ever rule under this roof."

—*John Adams*

Exciting Entry

On this day in 1956, Akio Toyoda was born. He is the grandson of Toyota's founder and is currently the president of the corporation. He was president when the company recalled 8.5 million vehicles.

Prominent Passing

On this day in 1724, John Leverett the Younger died. He was Harvard's first secular president and helped keep the college growing. He was president when Harvard established its first endowed chair.

While John Adams was the second president of the United States, he was the first president to live in the White House. On November 1, 1800, Adams moved into the President's House, now known as the White House.

Adams, near the end of his term, eventually decided to move into the White House. Although the house was habitable, construction was not yet finished. When Adams arrived, he found much of his own house's furniture already in place and a portrait of Washington hanging on the wall.

As the location was still growing, it took a long time for other fixtures to arrive. However, new carpeting, cabinets, tables, china, and other things were purchased for the Adams's during their stay.

Abigail Adams moved to the White House to be with her husband. However, they soon discovered that the winter made the house a damp, cold place to live. She attempted to remedy the situation by closing doors and keeping fires lit in every room, but to no avail.

Abigail Adams did, however, furnish some of the rooms enough to hold a New Year's Day reception in one of the rooms. This New Year's Day reception started a tradition that every president kept until 1932. Her work also helped make the White House not just a place for business, but a home.

May 4 — JEFFERSON'S BOOK COLLECTION

To Thomas Jefferson, books were extremely important, and he amassed a large number of books. His collection was considered the largest personal library in the United States at the time.

During the War of 1812, the British burned Washington D.C. and the Library of Congress was also destroyed. Jefferson's library of 6,487 volumes was offered to help rebuild the library's book collection, and Congress accepted, buying the entire collection for $23,950 in 1815.

Jefferson's collection actually doubled the Library of Congress's book holding that it lost in the fire. Before sending them to Washington, D.C., Jefferson packed up the books based on how he cataloged them.

Jefferson's catalog for his books went against the common practice of arranging the books alphabetically. He instead chose to model his library based by subject although in practice, it was based on the book's size. Many in Congress were skeptical of the purchase because many of Jefferson's books were in foreign languages or considered irrelevant to Congress.

Remarkable Remark

"I do not know that it [Jefferson's library] contains any branch of science which Congress would wish to exclude from their collection… [otherwise] Congress may not have occasion to refer [to it]."
—*Thomas Jefferson*

Exciting Entry

On this day in 1928, Hosni Mubarak was born. He became Egypt's president after President Sadat was murdered. Although tried for ordering protestors' deaths and for embezzlement, he was acquitted in 2017.

Prominent Passing

On this day in 1995, Lewis T. Preston died. Preston personally met with Mikhail Gorbachev and was president of the World Bank. He helped many of the former Soviet countries rebuild their economies.

Soon after Jefferson sold his books, he used the money to pay off loans and to rebuild his library. Congress used the books to restock the Library of Congress; however, a fire in 1851 destroyed two thirds of his collection, and the Library of Congress is currently trying to recreate his collection with editions that matched the original books.

May 5

MONROE'S FAITHLESS ELECTOR

To many, James Monroe was the ideal candidate. The start of his first term ushered in the Era of Good Feelings, and by the time his chance for reelection came, he ran virtually unopposed.

In the election of 1820, the Federalist Party had no official candidate, and the Republican Party did not oppose Monroe running for a second term. Because Monroe's re-election seemed inevitable, there was very little excitement surrounding the 1820 election. In Richmond, only seventeen people voted!

Monroe was able to win 231 of the 232 electoral votes in the election. The faithless elector, or an elector who goes against the wish of the people, was William Plumer of New Hampshire. Plumer voted for John Quincy Adams instead.

According to legend, Plumer voted against Monroe to allow Washington to be the only president unanimously voted in by the Electoral College. However, Plumer would not have known how every other elector would vote, and contemporary records show that Plumer voted against Monroe because he disliked Monroe's administration and was friends with Adams.

Newspapers from the time reported the incident correctly, and the legend did not come about until nearly sixty years later. Although Monroe lost one electoral vote, he still won by a resounding margin and continued the Era of Good Feelings throughout his second term as president.

May **6**

JACKSON'S DUELING WAY

Andrew Jackson, the seventh president of the United States of America, is remembered for his bombastic attitude and love of dueling.

Jackson participated in duels often because his wife, Rachel, who had unknowingly married Jackson before her divorce to her previous husband was finalized, had her honor insulted. Jackson challenged Charles Dickinson to a duel after he insulted Rachel.

While Jackson was a military man, Dickinson was considered the best shot in the area. People in the town even placed bets in favor of Dickinson.

Both men met on May 30, 1806, and Jackson arrived wearing a long loose coat. Dickinson fired first, breaking some of Jackson's ribs and lodging the bullet near his heart. However, the shot was not fatal because the jacket made it hard to precisely aim.

Jackson was able to remain standing and fired back as Dickinson, who according to dueling code, remained still. Ultimately, Jackson killed Dickinson. Many thought it was cold-blooded murder since they did not fire at the same time. However, Jackson shot based on the duel's rules.

Jackson survived, but the bullet that remained in his body often caused him great discomfort and pain. Although his killing Charles Dickinson made him unpopular for a time, Andrew Jackson was able to run a successful presidential campaign, and the duel did not affect his running for office.

Remarkable Remark
"As Dickinson…was certain of killing him at the first fire, he [Jackson] did not want him to have the gratification even of knowing that he had touched him [with the bullet]."
—*account of the Jackson-Dickinson duel*

Exciting Entry
On this day in 1758, Maximilien Robespierre was born. He was a leading member on the Committee of Public Safety and was president of the National Convention for roughly a month before being deposed.

Prominent Passing
On this day in 1840, Francisco de Paula Santander died. He served with Simón Bolívar during the South American revolutions and was president of the newly formed New Granada (Columbia) in the 1830s.

 **May 7**

THE FIRST MODERN CAMPAIGN

In the election of 1836, it was evident that Martin Van Buren would be president, and he won the election by a resounding margin. However, in the 1840 election, both Van Buren and his opponent, William Henry Harrison, ran very exciting campaigns.

Martin Van Buren's campaign was coming off of several national problems, and Van Buren was seeking to improve his image. Overall, Van Buren ran a normal, clean campaign, only occasionally attempting to slander Harrison.

William Henry Harrison was portrayed as the war hero from the Battle of Tippecanoe and took to the cities to gain voters' support. His followers wrote numerous campaign songs, including "Tippecanoe and Tyler Too," and rolled large paper balls, with campaign slogans written on it, through city streets while singing Harrison campaign songs.

When Van Buren supporters suggested Harrison should retire and live at his log cabin drinking cider, the Harrison side decided to embrace their idea. Harrison's campaign passed out hard cider in log cabin shaped bottles. They also portrayed Harrison as a man who grew up in a lowly log cabin, even though Harrison was from a wealthy Virginia family and grew up in a large house. Harrison's log cabin campaign and the numerous songs won him the election, and the election of 1840 is considered to be the first modern campaign.

HARRISON'S MEDICAL DIAGNOSIS

William Henry Harrison was the ninth president of the United States. He was a hero of the War of 1812 and is famous for his victory at Tippecanoe against the Indian chieftain Tecumseh's Indian coalition.

However, Harrison is more famous for a totally different reason. He was the first president to die in office. He delivered his inaugural address in inclement weather without a coat or hat to protect him. It was also the longest inaugural address given by a president and lasted roughly two hours.

Subsequently, he fell ill, and it was reported by Harrison's doctor, Thomas Miller, that the president had contracted pneumonia. Although Miller was not completely satisfied with the diagnosis, it explained the president's sudden illness.

However, some modern analysis has questioned if it was actually pneumonia and considered the possibility of it actually being typhoid fever. Harrison's water supply at the White House was near a marsh created by human excrement which could have easily contaminated the water in the White House. Regardless, the resulting medical treatment further weakened the president, and he died after being in office about a month.

Harrison's death forced the United States to consider who would succeed him. Under the Twelfth Amendment, Congress determined that Harrison's vice president, John Tyler, would become president.

Remarkable Remark

"The disease was not viewed as a case of pure pneumonia; but…the term pneumonia afforded a succinct…answer to the innumerable questions as to the nature of the attack."
—*Thomas Miller*

Exciting Entry

On this day in 1824, William Walker was born. He was an American revolutionary that became president of Nicaragua until he surrendered to the US Navy and returned to the United States.

Prominent Passing

On this day in 1997, Kai-Uwe von Hassel died. Kai-Uwe von Hassel was president of the Bundestag from 1969 to 1972 and the president of the European Union of Christian Democrats from 1973 to 1980.

TYLER'S SHORT GENEALOGY

Exciting Entry

On this day in 1926, Robin Cooke was born. He was a judge for over two decades and president of New Zealand's Appeal Court for ten years. He was considered one of New Zealand's preeminent judges.

Prominent Passing

On this day in 2016, John Warr died. He was a famous cricket player and was president of the Marylebone Cricket Club for a year. The MCC is the supreme judge of the Laws of cricket around the globe.

John Tyler, the United States of America's tenth president, was born in 1790, one year after Washington took office. He assumed the presidency in 1841 following William Harrison's death. However, Tyler's grandsons are actually still alive!

President Tyler married twice. The first time was to a woman named Letitia Christian Tyler, and he had several children with her. She died in 1842 after suffering a stroke. President Tyler then secretly married Julia Gardiner in 1844. She was thirty years his younger. She also had several children including Lyon Gardiner Tyler in 1853, when John Tyler was sixty-three.

Lyon Gardiner Tyler was born after his father had left office. Lyon, a college president and historian, also married twice. His first marriage was to Annie Baker Tucker, who died in 1921 and gave him three children. In 1923, Lyon Tyler married his second wife named Susan Ruffin Tyler, who had three children.

Lyon Tyler's children were born when he was in his seventies. They were Lyon Gardiner Tyler Jr., born in 1924, and Harrison Ruffin Tyler, born in 1928. Both sons are still alive, and Harrison takes care of John Tyler's house, along with his son. They have given interviews, and Harrison occasionally gives tours at his grandfather's house. That means that in three generations of Tyler's family, almost every major historical event and invention had occurred.

THE MANY NAMES OF JAMES K. POLK

May 10

James Polk, the eleventh president of the United States, reduced tariffs, added new states and territories, and led the country during the Mexican American War. His hard work also led to many nicknames.

Because Polk was relatively obscure outside of political spheres, he was labeled a "Dark Horse" candidate, or someone not expected to win. His opponents used the slogan "Who is James K. Polk?" in an effort to remind the people he was not well-known. Polk eventually won the election with 49.5% of the popular vote.

James Polk was also given the nickname "Young Hickory." His mentor, Andrew Jackson, held the nickname "Old Hickory," and Polk's nickname was an effort to tie the two together. What Jackson had in mind for the federal government, his protégé "Young Hickory" often carried out in the decisions he made as president.

One nickname of Polk's that many people have forgotten is "Napoleon of the Stump." In rural districts in the early 1800s, many politicians would give "stump" speeches. These speeches were often entertaining speeches that kept the crowd interested, and the speaker would often stand on a stump to be better heard. Polk's short stature and his popular speeches in his early career is how he earned the nickname "Napoleon of the Stump." Other nicknames Polk gained included "Polk the Plodder" and "Polk the Mendacious."

Remarkable Remark

"I regard the question of annexation as belonging exclusively to the United States and Texas. ...Foreign powers do not seem to appreciate the true character of our Government."
—*Polk's Inaugural Address*

Exciting Entry

On this day in 1926, Sir Duncan Watson was born. He was blind and served as president of the World Blind Union from 1988 to 1992. He worked as an advocate for the blind and for others with disabilities.

Prominent Passing

On this day in 1902, John S. Case died. He served as the mayor of Rockland, Maine, for four terms and in the legislature for four years. He was also the president of the Rockland National Bank.

 **May 11**

"I KNOW NOTHING"

Exciting Entry

On this day in 1911, Sir Edgar Beck was born. Beck was president of the British engineering company John Mowlem, which was responsible for restoring many of Britain's prominent public buildings.

Prominent Passing

On this day in 1996, Nnamdi Azikiwe died. Azikiwe was the first president of independent Nigeria. He was also president of several sports organizations, including football, boxing, and table tennis.

Millard Fillmore became the thirteenth president following President Zachary Taylor's death, serving the rest of Taylor's term. Not being reelected, Fillmore ran with a party most people know nothing about—the Know-Nothing Party.

The Know-Nothing Party came about following a rise in immigration to the United States in the 1840s. They were fiercely anti-immigration and anti-Catholic. Started as the Order of the Star-Spangled Banner, members were required to state that they "knew nothing" about the secret society.

As more members were added, the society eventually was renamed as the American Party, or the Know-Nothing Party. They wanted only American-born citizens in office, Bible reading in classrooms, and immigrants to wait twenty-one years to gain citizenship. By 1855, the Know-Nothing Party had forty-three party members in Congress.

The Know-Nothing Party's success led them to nominate Millard Fillmore as their presidential candidate. In the election of 1856, Democrat James Buchanan, Republican John Fremont, and American Millard Fillmore were the major candidates. Ultimately, Buchanan won the 1856 election, and Fillmore only won Maryland, signaling the end of the American Party's power. The American Party lost over two dozen seats in Congress, and by the Civil War, the Know-Nothing Party was essentially nonexistent.

WORTH ITS WEIGHT IN GOLD!

Franklin Pierce, the fourteenth president of the United States, is remembered for the Gadsden Purchase which created the modern day continental United States. However, most people do not realize that America's drive for new land expanded into the Pacific Ocean and how America obtained the land in a unique way.

In the 1840s, farmers across the United States were using a special fertilizer to improve their crops. This fertilizer was called guano, which is literally bird or bat excrement. In 1850, President Millard Fillmore told Congress that Peruvian guano was valuable to America. Peruvian guano made 67% of all of Peru's exports to Great Britain in 1870!

In 1856, President Franklin Pierce, recognizing that guano was essential to American farmers (especially since farmers now had more land to farm) signed the Guano Islands Act. In the 1850s, four pounds of guano cost roughly the same amount as one pound of gold! This act would allow the United States greater access to guano at a greatly reduced price.

Remarkable Remark
"Whenever any citizen of the United States discovers a deposit of guano on any island, rock, or key… [the island can] be considered as appertaining to the United States."
—48 US Code Chapter 8

Exciting Entry
On this day in 1936, Guillermo Endara was born. He became the president of Panama after the United States deposed Manuel Noriega. Endara is credited with bringing democracy back to the country of Panama.

Prominent Passing
On this day in 1992, Joe Burke died. Burke was a baseball executive for decades and president of the Kansas City Royals from 1981 to 1992. He was selected major league executive of the year in 1976.

The Guano Island Act allowed any US citizen to claim an uninhabited or unclaimed island as long as there was guano on the island. This act allowed the US government to lay claim to roughly one hundred islands, including Howland and Baker Island. The Guano Islands Act is in the law books as 48 US Code Chapter 8 and is still a valid law.

 **May 13**

BUCHANAN'S MYSTERIOUS ILLNESS

James Buchanan was the United States' fifteenth president and is generally considered to be one of the worst presidents. However, what most people do not realize is that just before he was sworn in, Buchanan almost died.

At the time, presidents were sworn in in March instead of January, and president elects would often arrive in Washington D.C. early. Buchanan arrived early and stayed at the National Hotel, one of the city's most elegant hotels.

When Buchanan went to the National Hotel, he was in Washington for meetings and to finalize his choices for his Cabinet. Buchanan fell ill and went home sick, eventually recovering some weeks later.

Not only did Buchanan fall ill, several congressmen also became seriously ill. Eventually, nearly forty people died. The newspapers in the area immediately began proclaiming that Buchanan had been poisoned in an attempt to assassinate the incoming president. Meanwhile, the mayor and others attempted to quell the rumors, but to no avail. The breakout of illness was later called the "National Hotel Disease," and although many people claimed it was an attempted assassination on Buchanan's life, it was ultimately determined that the illness was dysentery that was most likely caused by a sewage problem. The National Hotel was destroyed in the 1940s, and a museum is located where it used to be.

LINCOLN'S FINAL JOURNEY

Abraham Lincoln led the nation through the Civil War and is considered to be one of America's best presidents. However, in the nearly forty years after his death, his body was moved over a dozen times to keep it safe.

Lincoln's death train carried both Lincoln and his son, William, and traveled 1,600 miles with over 400 stops. Eventually, Lincoln's body arrived in Springfield, Illinois, where he was laid to rest in Oak Ridge Cemetery.

From 1865 to 1874, Lincoln's body was moved four times while Lincoln's tomb was being built. In November of 1876, counterfeiters attempted to steal Lincoln's body and hold it for ransom. However, a Secret Service agent that had infiltrated the group alerted the police, and the robbery was unsuccessful.

In the rest of November of 1876, Lincoln's body was moved four more times in an attempt to keep his location a secret and his body safe from robberies. In 1878, he was moved twice, once in response to an anonymous threat.

Remarkable Remark

"I watched the shadow of the lid fall across Lincoln's face as that face disappeared from mortal view forever."
—B. H. Monroe on viewing Lincoln

Exciting Entry

On this day in 1906, Hastings Kamuzu Banda was born. Banda was the first president of Malawi, formerly Nyasaland, and ruled with a mix of totalitarian control and conservative economic policies.

Prominent Passing

On this day in 1945, Heber Grant died. He was the seventh president of the Church of Jesus Christ of Latter-Day Saints. He supported the League of Nations and was sad when Utah repealed prohibition.

From 1887 to 1901, Lincoln's body was moved six times while a more permanent location was being built. Lincoln's body was viewed several times throughout his many moves to quell rumors that the body was not actually Lincoln. On September 26, 1901, Lincoln's body was interred for the final time in a steel cage under ten feet of concrete, never again to be disturbed.

 **May 15**

JOHNSON'S ATTEMPT ASSASSINATION

Many remember Andrew Johnson for his Reconstruction policies and impeachment, but few remember he was almost killed the same night Lincoln was shot.

John Wilkes Booth had two fellow conspirators that were assigned to kill the vice president and the secretary of state. George Atzerdot, the man tasked with killing Andrew Johnson, was a German-born immigrant that had helped pro-Confederates in the area.

On the evening of April 14, Atzerdot was to assassinate Johnson at the Kirkwood Hotel. Unable to gain enough courage to take a man's life for no reason, Atzerdot drank, attempting to find the nerve to kill. However, he could not kill Johnson in cold blood and instead left the hotel and wandered the streets of Washington D.C., eventually going to his cousin's house.

After Lincoln was assassinated, an hotel employee contacted the police regarding a suspicious man. A search of Atzerdot's room revealed a gun, knife, and other suspicious items. Atzerdot was captured five days later at his cousin's home in Maryland.

Atzerdot was held on a ship at the Washington Navy Yard and later at the Old Arsenal Penitentiary. He was tried along with the other conspirators, and his defense team attempted to prove he was merely a coward who played no role in the assassination attempts. Atzerdot was sentenced to death and was hung on July 7, 1865. His burial place remains a mystery.

May 16 — GRANT'S MEMOIRS

Ulysses Grant was the eighteenth president of the United States and a hero of the Civil War. However, after his presidency, Grant went into business to support his family.

Because presidents did not receive a salary after they left office until the 1950s, many presidents had to go back to work follow-ing their time in office. To try to earn enough money to support his family, Grant began writing his memoirs and was going to publish it with a magazine company before Mark Twain's publishing company got the deal.

Grant signed a contract with Twain's company (Charles L. Webster and Company) and received a small advance. Twain decided to sell Grant's memoirs as a two-volume set and mapped out the United States into sixteen divisions to better maximize the books capability of selling. Grant, also dying of cancer, was attempting to finish his memoirs to provide for his family.

While battling cancer and trying to write his memoirs, Grant had to deal with a disloyal helper in his book project, people assuming Twain actually wrote the book, Congress denying him a pension, and his illness becoming public and sensationalized.

Grant finished his book, *The Personal Memoirs of U.S. Grant*, just before he died, and Mark Twain was able to give Grant's wife a royalty check from the book soon thereafter that would provide for Grant's family for many years.

Remarkable Remark

"It was a shameful thing that a man who had saved this coun-try..from destruction should still be in a po-sition where so small a sum...could be looked upon as a godsend."

—Mark Twain

Exciting Entry

On this day in 1916, Ephraim Katzir was born. He was an Israeli scientist and was the first Israeli elected to the US Na-tional Academy of Sci-ences. He also served as Israel's fourth president.

Prominent Passing

On this day in 1977, Mod-ibo Keita died. He was Mali's president for most of the 1960s and closely aligned with Communist countries to help carry out his socialist policies until he was overthrown.

May 17

HAYES:
A MAN OF MANY FIRSTS

Exciting Entry
On this day in 1942, Myles Brand was born. He was president of the University of Oregon and the University of Indiana. He also served as president of the National Collegiate Athletic Association.

Prominent Passing
On this day in 1879, Asa Packer died. Packer built the Lehigh Valley Railroad and was its president when he died. He also served in Congress and founded Lehigh University in Bethlehem, Pennsylvania.

Rutherford B. Hayes was the nineteenth president of the United States and is mostly a forgotten US president. However, Hayes's presidency was filled with many firsts.

In the election of 1876, Hayes became the first and only president to be chosen by congressional commission. Because the election had several inconsistencies and disputed electoral votes, the election was decided by a congressional commission. The committee gave Hayes the victory over Samuel Tilden. The close election and the resulting commission led Hayes to gain the nickname "Rutherfraud."

Rutherford B. Hayes also was the first president to take the Oath of Office at the White House on March 3 because election day, March 4, was a Sunday. In 1880, Hayes was also the first president to visit the West Coast when he took a cross-country tour by train. He was also the first president to allow women to argue cases before the Supreme Court and to keep an alcohol-free White House.

Hayes also hosted the first White House Easter Egg Roll in 1878, an annual event at the White House that has only stopped briefly around the times of WWI and WWII. Hayes was also the first president to have a telephone installed and a typewriter used in the White House. Rutherford Hayes was the first president to graduate from law school, and Lucy Hayes was the first First Lady to have graduated from college.

May 18

GARFIELD'S COMICAL NOMINATION

James Garfield was the twentieth president of the United States. However, his path to the presidential nomination was a surprise even to himself.

The Republican National Convention in 1880 originally had three main candidates. General Ulysses Grant, Maine's Senator James G. Blaine, and Secretary of the Treasury John Sherman, whom Garfield supported.

The convention remained in a deadlock on Saturday and refused to attempt to nominate a president on Sunday.

On Monday, twenty-eight ballots were cast attempting to nominate a president, but to no avail. The next morning, Garfield received a note from a powerful political boss suggesting that Garfield might become the dark horse candidate (someone not expected to be nominated), but Garfield replied that his loyalty remained with Sherman.

However, during the voting Tuesday, the states quickly began voting for Garfield, who was still adamantly opposed to the idea. Instead of Garfield occasionally receiving a few votes on each ballot, suddenly whole state delegations were voting for him. Garfield won the nomination on the thirty-sixth ballot and went on to become president. The balloting began with a majority for Grant and ended with Garfield as the nominee. Garfield was against his name being voted for without his consent, but once nominated, he willingly ran for president, considering it an honor.

Remarkable Remark

"I wish you would say that this is no act of mine. I wish you would say that I have done everything and omitted nothing to secure Secretary Sherman's nomination."
—Garfield's reply to being nominated

Exciting Entry

On this day in 1885, Eurico Gaspar Dutra was born. Dutra was president of Brazil from 1945 to 1950 and worked to improve relations with the United States. He also returned Brazil to democratic rule.

Prominent Passing

On this day in 2014, Dobrica Ćosić died. He was president of Yugoslavia from 1992 to 1993. He campaigned for Serbian rights within Yugoslavia and was considered by some the father of the nation.

MCKINLEY'S DEATH

Exciting Entry

On this day in 1858, Prince Roland Napoléon Bonaparte was born. He was related to Napoleon Bonaparte and was president of the French Société de Géographie, the world's oldest geographic society.

Prominent Passing

On this day in 1901, Marthinus Pretorius died. He was a Boer statesman and became president of both the South African Republic and the Orange Free State. Pretoria, South Africa is named after him.

William McKinley was the twenty-fifth president of the United States and served nearly one term before being assassinated by an anarchist.

In 1901, President William McKinley was shot by an anarchist of Polish descent. Leon Czolgosz approached McKinley with a gun hidden in a handkerchief and fired two shots into the president's chest before being taken to the ground by McKinley's bodyguards.

President McKinley surreptitiously wore a red carnation as a "good luck" charm. He won several congressional elections and the presidency while wearing one. On the day he was assassinated, McKinley gave a young child the carnation moments before being shot.

In October of 1901, an unremorseful Czolgosz was executed by the electric chair. His execution was allegedly filmed by none other than Thomas Edison, who was very interested in the killing ability of electricity.

Part of the reason that Czolgosz was able to get so close to President McKinley was that there was no official Secret Service exclusively for the protection of the president. The Secret Service at that time was a branch of the Treasury Department that mainly investigated counterfeiting. Following the shooting of McKinley, the Secret Service officially started protecting the president. Their first task was guarding the new president, Theodore Roosevelt.

ROOSEVELT TRAGIC VALENTINES DAY

Theodore Roosevelt was the twenty-sixth president of the United States. While his presidency was memorable to many, Roosevelt suffered tragedy early on in his political career.

To many, Valentine's Day is a day to celebrate love. However, it was not so for Theodore Roosevelt on that fateful Thursday, February 14, 1884. On that day, both his wife and mother died within hours of each other in the same house.

Roosevelt's wife, Alice, who had just given birth to their daughter, was ill with Bright's disease, a severe kidney disorder. His mother, Mittie, had been battling typhoid fever. Roosevelt, currently serving in the New York state legislature, rushed home from Albany to be with them when he heard the news.

Shortly after Theodore arrived, his mother died from typhoid fever, and roughly eleven hours later, he watched as his wife died from Bright's disease. In his diary that day, Roosevelt's entry reflected the grief he was feeling.

Remarkable Remark

"The light has gone out of my life."
—*Theodore Roosevelt's journal entry for February 14, 1884*

Exciting Entry

On this day in 1935, José Mujica was born. He was president of Uruguay from 2010 to 2015 and helped Uruguay's economy to prosper. Under his presidency, Uruguay also passed progressive legislation.

Prominent Passing

On this day in 1939, Joe Carr died. He was president of the NFL from 1921 to 1939 and helped shape the NFL into the league it is today. He was enshrined into the Pro Football Hall of Fame in 1963.

Roosevelt prohibited others from mentioning his wife's name and told a friend that the pain he felt would destroy him if he did not work to move on. This day was also the four-year anniversary of Teddy and Alice's engagement. Sadly, it was filled with sadness for this great man. Roosevelt left politics and went out West for several years before returning to New York and politics.

May 21

UNTOLD STORY OF BILLY POSSUM

Exciting Entry

On this day in 1944, Mary Robinson was born. She was Ireland's first female president and served from 1990 to 1997. She also traveled extensively around the globe as a strong supporter of human rights.

Prominent Passing

On this day in 1920, Venustiano Carranza died. Carranza was president of Mexico from 1917 to 1920 and helped keep Mexico neutral during WWI. He was killed while fleeing from those in opposition to him.

Although William Taft was the twenty-seventh president of the United States, he preferred being recognized for his service on the Supreme Court. Taft also had a toy made in honor of him, but this is forgotten to have existed by most people.

The toy market was a newer industry at the time and was quickly becoming a major industry. Theodore Roosevelt had a stuffed bear named after him, but many people at the time believed the Teddy Bear would only be a fad.

At a dinner one night, Taft ate a meal consisting of an eighteen-pound opossum and sweet potatoes. Following the meal, Taft was presented with a stuffed opossum, nicknamed Billy Possum. The stuffed animal was supposed to become the next Teddy Bear, which was expected to flop once Roosevelt left office.

The Georgia Billy Possum Company formed, and thousands of stuffed possums were soon made. The advertising campaigns suggested getting rid of your teddy bears and buying the latest and greatest—Billy Possum.

Possum clubs began to form, and the Jimmie Possum was created, based off Taft's running mate, James Sherman. Songs, postcards, pins, and more were created to sell the new toy. However, Billy Possum was a flop, and the Teddy Bear reigned supreme, largely because Roosevelt's toy was based on emotions while Taft's was based on his appetite.

 **THE SECRET PRESIDENT**

Woodrow Wilson was the twenty-eighth president of the United States and led the US through WWI. However, the strain of war weighed heavy on Wilson, and for the final few months of his life, it was not Wilson who was really running the country.

From late 1918 to early 1919, Wilson was in Europe finalizing the League of Nations and the Treaty of Versailles. His endless work quickly tired him, and his September cross-country trip attempting to get US support for the league only hurt his condition.

Wilson, never a healthy man, only got worse during his trip. Wilson suffered a small stroke on the journey, and the rest of his cross-country speaking tour was canceled. In October, the president woke to find himself partially paralyzed and unable to work.

Uncertain if the presidential power should be given to the vice president, and unwilling to let her husband lose his power, Edith Wilson essentially ran the government for her husband. Keeping the extent of his illness from the public, Congress, and the Cabinet, Edith was able to successfully keep her husband as president. While she proclaimed Woodrow was completely able to perform his duties as president and that she played a very small role, recent research has concluded that she really was running the government, minus major decisions and new programs, until her husband's second term ended in 1921.

Remarkable Remark
"So began my steward-ship...The only decision that was mine was what was important and what was not, and the very important decision of when to present matters to my husband."
—*Edith Wilson*

Exciting Entry
On this day in 1891, Robert Gordon Sproul was born. He served as president of the University of California (UCLA) from 1930 to 1958. Although a university president, Sproul only had a bachelors degree.

Prominent Passing
On this day in 1540, Francesco Guicciardini died. He was a historian and worked closely with the Medici family and the Papacy. In 1524, he was appointed president of the Romagna, a papal province.

COOLIDGE'S CREATURE COMPOUND

Remarkable Remark

"A great many presents come to the White House, which are all cherished, not so much for their intrinsic value as because they are tokens of esteem and affection."

—Coolidge on his many animals

Exciting Entry

On this day in 1874, Alfred P. Sloan Jr. was born. He was president and chairman of General Motors for over twenty-five years. He helped restructure the company and helped it dominate the market in car sales.

Prominent Passing

On this day in 2009, Roh Moo-Hyun died. He was a lawyer and served as president of South Korea from 2003 to 2008. His presidency was plagued with scandal and he was impeached but later reinstated.

Calvin Coolidge was the thirtieth president of the United States. Known for his quiet witticism, Coolidge also collected a unique menagerie of animals.

The Coolidge family had roughly a dozen dogs that roamed the property. Mrs. Coolidge enjoyed taking photographs with her dogs and even made calling cards for some of them. Their two white collies, however, were quite possibly their favorite animals.

In 1926, the Coolidges were sent a raccoon from Mississippi that was supposed to be eaten for Thanksgiving. However, the president "pardoned" the animal and named it Rebecca, letting it live with the family until she was sent to the zoo. They were also given another raccoon, named Rueben, but Rebecca and Rueben did not get along.

The Coolidges owned three canaries, a goose named Enoch, and a mockingbird. They also owned two cats, a bobcat named Smoky, and a donkey named Ebenezer. They even were given several exotic animals, including a wallaby, black bear, and two lion cubs. Coolidge named the two lion cubs Tax Reduction and Budget Bureau.

They also recieved a pygmy hippo named Billy. It was a gift from tire magnate Harvey Samuel Firestone, and when the president received the gift, he immediately donated the hippo to the National Zoo. The hippo became a larger attraction then even the monkeys and traveled to the 1939 New York World's Fair.

 *May* **24**

DID FDR USE AL CAPONE'S CAR?

On December 8, 1941, Franklin Delano Roosevelt took a car to the Capitol to give a speech to a joint session of Congress. This car, however, was no ordinary car as it was Al Capone's bulletproof car which was used to keep FDR safe. The only problem with this nice little trivia story is that it is only a myth.

One of FDR's secret service agents, Michael F. Reilly, wrote several books, and in one of them, he mentions the need for an armored car to protect the president while he traveled. However, Reilly states that they used the car on December 9th, not the 8th, and merely draped their bodies around the car and had the military line the streets.

His account, however, has several problems. One of which is that he called the car an open-top car, when Capone's car was a closed-top car. Another problem in his story was that at the time, Capone's car was on display in England, and several photos from December 8, 1941, clearly shows a different car than the one Al Capone owned. Books, bloggers, and even CBS all wrote about the story, but they are not true.

Remarkable Remark

"Yesterday, December 7, 1941—a date which will live in infamy—the United States of America was suddenly and deliberately attacked by…the Empire of Japan."
—*Franklin Delano Roosevelt*

Exciting Entry

On this day in 1884, Walter Franklin was born. At one time or another, he was president of the Detroit, Toledo & Ironton Railroad; Wabash Railroad; Pennsylvania Railroad; and Long Island Railroad.

Prominent Passing

On this day in 1907, John Patton Jr. died. A US senator, he served as president of the State League of Republican Clubs and later as president of the Board of Library Commissioners of Grand Rapids.

While the president's usual car, his "Sunshine Special," was being refitted to protect him, what FDR really used during this time was a 1938 semi-armored Cadillac from the White House Fleet. So, contrary to popular opinion, FDR did not ride in Al Capone's car on that fateful day in 1941, but in one of his own government vehicles.

AN ATTEMPT ON PRESIDENT TRUMAN'S LIFE

When Harry Truman became the thirty-third president, he spent several years at the nearby Blair House instead of the White House because of renovations.

While Truman lived at the Blair House, two Puerto Rican nationals, Oscar Collazo and Griselio Torresola, who wanted an independent Puerto Rico, decided that assassinating the president would shed light on their cause. They went to the capital for the purpose of killing the president.

On November 1, 1950, as Truman was taking an afternoon nap, a gunfight between the two assassins, White House guards, and the Secret Service broke out. Truman, who was woken by the fighting, looked out the window overlooking the fight until a guard yelled at him to get down, which he quickly did.

In the gunfight, Secret Service agent Leslie Coffelt was mortally wounded, but before he died, he shot and killed Torresola. Two other officers were wounded multiple times but later recovered. The other assassin was arrested and sentenced to death, but a week before he was to die, Truman commuted his sentence to life imprisonment and President Carter commuted his life sentence so that Collazo went free.

In the aftermath of the attempted assassination, Congress passed a law expanding Secret Service protection to the president, his family, and the president elect.

LBJ, A WORLD WAR II HERO?

At the outbreak of WWII, many young Americans joined the military to do their part in defeating the enemy. Many prominent Americans and future leaders also joined the military. One such man was then Congressman Lyndon Baine Johnson.

Lyndon Johnson was a lieutenant commander in the Naval Reserve, even though he had no formal training. When America joined the Allies, Johnson reported for active duty soon after Pearl Harbor, and President Roosevelt assigned Johnson to observe military actions in the Pacific Theater and report back to him.

While there, he swayed General Douglass MacArthur to let him join a bombing mission as an observer; however, prior to takeoff, he left his airplane to use the restroom. When he returned, his seat was taken, and he flew on a different plane.

During the mission, the plane he was supposed to be on was shot down with no survivors. The plane he was on had electrical problems and returned to base under heavy fire. Johnson was awarded a controversial Silver Star by General MacArthur for remaining calm and returning alive with valuable information, and he proudly displayed the medal the rest of his life. However, the actual soldiers who flew the plane never received a reward for their bravery, and more recent researchers believe the entire story to be made up.

Remarkable Remark
"For gallantry in action… in the Southwest Pacific area, Lieutenant Commander Johnson…volunteered as an observer on a hazardous aerial combat mission over hostile positions."
—LBJ's medal citation

Exciting Entry
On this day in 1910, Adolpho López Mateos was born. He was president of Mexico from 1958 to 1964 and expanded Mexico's industrialization while increasing the government's control over the economy.

Prominent Passing
On this day in 1943, Edsel Ford died. He became president of Ford Motor Company in 1918, but his dad Henry Ford really retained power. Edsel bought the Lincoln Motor Company and became its president.

NIXON HONORS VIETNAM POWS

Exciting Entry

On this day in 1738, Nathaniel Gorham was born. A member of the Continental Congress, Gorham served one year as president. He later attended the Constitutional Convention and signed the Constitution.

Prominent Passing

On this day in 1964, Jawaharlal Nehru died. Nehru was the president of India's Congress Party and helped lead the way for India's independence. He was also independent India's first prime minister.

While President Richard Nixon is best remembered for the Watergate Scandal, he also worked on numerous national and international problems with great success. One issue he dealt with was the end of American involvement in the Vietnam War and the return of hundreds of Vietnam prisoners of war.

President Nixon decided to honor the nearly six hundred prisoners of war that had been safely returned to the United States by giving them a banquet. He had a tent, that by some accounts was larger than the White House, installed on the South Lawn, and he had each table set up as fancy as a state dinner with the expensive White House china.

Roughly 1,300 guests attended and were served roast beef sirloin, seafood Neptune, and strawberry mousse. Several famous guests also attended, including John Wayne, Jimmy Stewart, Bob Hope, and Irving Berlin. The soldiers gave President Nixon a plaque in recognition of his work in getting them released from Vietnam.

A group of POWs sang their POW hymn that was written and composed by pilot James Quincy Collins, who wrote it with a fishbone while being held a prisoner. The president greeted each soldier cordially and made sure they all had a good time, and the POWs were allowed to tour the entire White House without restrictions and stay as long as they wanted. Forty years later, the remaining POWs met again to celebrate the event.

 **FORD THE CO-PRESIDENT?**

While Gerald Ford was the first vice president and president never to be elected into office, he was also almost the co-president of the United States.

After Ford finished his term in office, he withdrew from the political sphere until Ronald Reagan ran for president. It was during this time that Ford began to seriously consider being Reagan's vice president in name, while a co-president in action.

While Reagan finally choose George H. W. Bush as his vice president, Reagan only choose him after disagreeing with the proposed presidential plan put forth by Ford. Reagan did not approve of Ford and his policies; however, he was the perfect running mate to win the election as it brought together a large number of voters.

Ford wanted to be in control of several key positions and have the power to appoint several leading foreign policy officials. Ford was so confident of his opportunity to be co-president that he went on national television prior to Reagan officially selecting his running mate and affirmed by not denying that they were discussing a co-presidency.

Remarkable Remark
"Gerald Ford will be his [Reagan's] selection as his vice-presidential running mate....They are going...to announce that Ford will run with him."
—*news anchor Walter Cronkite*

Exciting Entry
On this day in 1884, Edvard Beneš was born. Beneš was Czechoslovakia's president before and after World War II and continued to serve as president when the government was in exile in Great Britain.

Prominent Passing
On this day in 1873, Thomas Brown Anderson died. He was a Montreal merchant and served as a director, vice president, and president of the Bank of Montreal, serving as president from 1860 to 1869.

Ultimately, Reagan and Ford could not agree, and Reagan chose George H. W. Bush instead for his vice president. Bush agreed to fully support some of Reagan's major beliefs and practices, such as Reaganomics and his stance on abortion, things he had previously been against fully supporting.

JIMMY CARTER'S NOBEL PEACE PRIZE

Exciting Entry

On this day in 1917, John F. Kennedy was born. He was the youngest US president elected into office, but the youngest president was Teddy Roosevelt. JFK was the youngest president to die in office.

Prominent Passing

On this day in 2011, Sergei Bagapsh died. He was president of Abkhazia and worked to gain international recognition for Abkhazian independence from the Trans-caucasian country of Georgia, but to no avail.

Jimmy Carter was America's thirty-ninth president and was known for mediating a peace agreement between Israeli Prime Minister Menachem Begin and Egyptian president Anwar Sadat. The Camp David Peace Accords was President Carter's foreign policy highlight and helped paved the way to his earning the Nobel Peace Prize.

After his term in office, Jimmy Carter remained active in the political sphere, using his foreign policy experience in different avenues. He founded the Carter Center, which focused on promoting human rights, something Cater promoted as president, and democratic ideals. He also worked with Habitat for Humanity International helping to build houses for poor families across the globe.

Carter also helped as a mediator between the US government and several major world leaders, including Kim Il Sung of North Korea and Muammar al-Qaddafi of Libya. His decades of service mediating peace and advancing social standards provided the basis for his Nobel Prize nomination.

Because Jimmy Carter spent much of his time promoting peace and enhancing social living standards, he received the Nobel Peace Prize in 2002 in economics for his lifelong work in promoting international peace and economic develpment.

RONALD REAGAN'S JELLY BEANS

To most, Ronald Reagan was the movie actor turned president that helped end the Cold War. However, he did have a lighter side, whic included his love for jelly beans.

Ronald Reagan began eating Goelitz Mini Jelly Beans when he first ran for California governor. He used the snack as a way to beat his habit of pipe smoking, eating a handfull anytime he got the urge to smoke. This helped him slowly wean himself off his habit.

Reagan's smoking habit eventually dissipated, but his love for jelly beans did not. Reagan recieved a monthly shipment during his time as governor and even had a special jar designed especially for him.

After he left the governorship, he continued getting a shipment of jelly beans from the company. During his presidential campaign, Reagan continued eating his favorite snack, and he could often be seen passing around a bowl of jelly beans on trips and at meetings.

At Reagan's inauguration, the company sent three and a half tons of red, white, and blue jelly beans to the capitol to be shaped into a flag for the inauguration. The government even approved the company to make special jars of jelly beans with the presidential seal, which would then be handed out to foreign leaders and White House guests. There are even several portraits of Reagan made out of jelly beans. Reagan's favorite flavor was licorice.

Remarkable Remark
"They have become such a tradition of this Administration that it's gotten to the point where we can hardly start a meeting or make a decision without passing around the jar of jelly beans."
—*Ronald Reagan*

Exciting Entry
On this day in 1919, René Ortuño was born. Ortuño was Bolivia's president. He led a successful military coup, survived multiple assassination attempts, and defended his regime from revolutionaries.

Prominent Passing
On this day in 1994, Ezra Benson died. Benson was the Mormon Church's president and was the agriculture secretary for Eisenhower. He received the Presidential Citizens Medal from George H. W. Bush.

BUSH'S "CHICKEN KIEV" SPEECH

Remarkable Remark

"Americans will not support those who seek in- dependence in order to replace a far-off tyranny with a local despotism. They will not aid those who promote a suicidal nationalism."

—*Bush Sr.*

Exciting Entry

On this day in 1883, Lauri Kristian Relander was born. He was Finland's second president and helped place the new republic on the international stage by inviting foreign dignitaries to visit Finland.

Prominent Passing

On this day in 1960, Walter Funk died. He was president of the Reichsbank and a forgotten member of Hitler's Nazi party. At Nuremburg, he was sentenced to life imprisonment but was released in 1957.

While many identify the forty-first president, George Herbert Walker Bush, as one of America's best more recent presidents, he also had a few political blunders.

As the Cold War came to an end, Bush toured several Soviet countries. It was during this time that Bush made a severe political blunder.

In Kiev, Ukraine, in 1991, just weeks before Ukraine declared themselves an independent state, Bush spoke before the Ukrainian parliament and warned them of "suicidal nationalism." He continued by saying the United States would not support replacing one tyranny with another.

Critics in Ukraine and the United States called his speech the "Chicken Kiev" speech because it took such a week stance on Communism and seemed to ignore the Ukrainians' drive for democracy at a critical time in the Cold War. Many of George Bush's political advisors feared that the speech would lose many Ukrainian American voters in upcoming elections. Congress also passed resolutions in support of Ukraine's endeavors for independence.

Bush eventually recognized Ukraine as a country and later clarified his statements by telling Ukrainian students he merely meant not to do anything stupid in the process for freedom. However, some historians then and now view it as a blemish on George H. W. Bush's record as president, regardless of what the president meant.

WESTERN EXPANSION

"The West" is often thought of as a time period following the Civil War, a time full of cowboys and Indians, farmers and ranchers, lawmen and outlaws. Yet western expansion was an American ideal since America's founding and remains more complex than one might think. America's western expansion spans hundreds of years and contains the stories of unique individuals who shaped America into what she is today.

Hundreds of thousands of people helped expand the Western frontier and many have been forgotten to history, but their influence is still seen. Men, women, and children of all nationalities, religions, and social classes came together to populate the American frontier and to help create the America we know today. This June, you will read about stories involving the Western Frontier, spanning from the earliest days of the American republic to the end of the "Old West." These people helped create a prosperous "New West" that was able to be enjoyed by all.

June **1**

DANIEL BOONE SETTLES TRANSYLVANIA

Remarkable Remark

"We were then in a dan-gerous, helpless situation, exposed daily to perils and death, amongst savages and wild beasts, not a white man in the country but ourselves."

—*Daniel Boone*

Exciting Entry

On this day in 1801, Brigham Young was born. Young was a Mormon pioneer and church leader that led the Mormons west to Utah, practiced polygamy against societal norms, and had around fifty wives!

Prominent Passing

On this day in 1887, Joseph Isaac (Ike) Clanton died. Clanton was one of the men involved at the shootout at the OK Corral; however, he survived by running away as soon as the shooting started.

The name Daniel Boone brings to mind a frontiersman wearing a coonskin cap, clearing the Wilderness Road, and fighting Indians to settle his own territory. However, Boone actually wore beaver hats and was going West to settle a new colony called Transylvania.

Boone was hired by the Transylvania Company of North Carolina in 1775 to clear a trail to the land the company had recently acquired. The company was made of nine wealthy, prominent men in North Carolina, including Richard Henderson.

Daniel Boone and nearly thirty other men worked at clearing a small, walkable trail from East Tennessee through the Cumberland Gap called the Wilderness Road. When the men reached their destination, Boone began to build a settlement he called Boonesborough. All of this occurred prior to and during the American War for Independence.

Eventually more settlers came, and Boone eventually settled in Boonesborough for many years with his family. When the Transylvania Company petitioned the Continental Congress for admission as the fourteenth colony, both Virginia and North Carolina objected and nothing ever came of it.

The Transylvania Company's idea of a new colony was dropped, and the area became known as Kentucky. Boone continued to move West, heading to present day West Virginia and Missouri where he died.

THE LOUISIANA PURCHASE

Following the Revolutionary War, very little new land was purchased or fought over by the United States to provide for the masses of people wanting to go West. However, in 1803, Charles Maurice de Talleyrand, the Foreign Minister of France, offered to sell all of the Louisiana Territory to the United States.

Napoleon Bonaparte was needing more money to finance his endeavors and the distant Louisiana Territory seemed like the perfect piece of real estate to profit from. Meanwhile, Thomas Jefferson was interested in purchasing the city of New Orleans to keep the Mississippi River free for American commerce.

The price of the land that is often quoted is $15 million; however, it was actually only $11.25 million in cash, while the other $3.75 million was forgiveness of French debt. But, even at the low price of three cents per acre, the United States was unable to pay the full amount up front. The transaction had to be handled by two European banks. Including interest, the total cost of the Louisiana Purchase was over $23 million.

Remarkable Remark

"Overnight, the upstart nation acquired land physically larger than France, Spain, Portugal, Italy, Holland, Switzerland, and the British Isles combined."
—*From* Financial Founding Fathers

Exciting Entry

On this day in 1891, Thurman Arnold was born. Arnold was the mayor of Laramie, Wyoming, his hometown. He was also the assistant attorney general for Franklin Delano Roosevelt's Antitrust Division.

Prominent Passing

On this day in 1901, Richard Cunningham McCormick died. He was appointed as the Arizona Territory's secretary in 1862, its governor in 1866, and served as its delegate to Congress from 1869 to 1875.

Although Jefferson was a strict constructionist, he authorized the negotiations despite there being no language in the Constitution allowing the government to make such a transaction. Despite being opposed by the loose-construction Federalist Party, the treaty was ratified, doubling the size of the United States.

June **3**

SACAGAWEA'S SON JEAN BAPTISTE

The Merriweather Lewis and William Clark expedition would probably not have been a great success without the aid of Sacagawea. Her guidance and knowledge was invaluable to the explorers, and she even took her baby son on the expedition, only adding to her heroic status on the journey.

Jean Baptiste Charbonneau was just a young baby when Sacagawea and her husband, Toussaint Charbonneau, joined the Lewis and Clark expedition. Sacagawea carried little Pomp or Pompey, as he was nicknamed, five thousand miles to the Pacific Ocean, including carrying him over the vast Rocky Mountains.

The young child and his mother proved helpful in a rather unusual way when meeting with Indian tribes. They were often met kindly because no attacking war party would bring a woman or a baby with them. The expedition loved "Little Pompey" so much that they even named a landform after him called Pompey's Pillar, which is located near Billings, Montana.

After the expedition parted with Sacagawea, William Clark offered to educate Pompey, as he had grown very fond of the child. Clark became his guardian and paid for him to have an excellent education. Pompey lived in Germany for several years before returning to the United States as a hunter, guide, and adventurer. He went to California trying to find gold and died in 1866 on his way to Montana, again looking for gold.

June **4**

THE FORGOTTEN
EXPLORER OF LOUISIANA

While many remember explorers like Merriweather Lewis, William Clark, and Zebulon Pike, few remember the name Thomas Freeman. Freeman led the Red River Expedition, or the "Grand Excursion," and was joined by Captain Richard Spark and naturalist Peter Custis.

The expedition took two years to plan, and Congress provided $5,000 for the trip, twice what Congress had provided for the Lewis and Clark expedition. They set off in 1806 and began making slow progress down the Red River. They were ordered to study the landscape, animals, and people and to document everything of interest.

The expedition consisted of fewer military men and more scientists and civilians to gather as much valuable information as possible. The group faced many hardships, including a logjam that was over 160 miles and took roughly two weeks to get around. The men also recorded several new animals and made friends with several Indian tribes. They even recorded catching catfish weighing seventy pounds!

However, because the Americans were exploring in a region with its borders still disputed, the Spanish sent soldiers to confront them. Jefferson had told the men to return if confronted by a larger force, therefore, Freeman turned back. They only made it about half way down the Red River in their four month expedition, and most have forgotten that this expedition ever occurred.

 **June 5**

DAVY CROCKETT'S BIRTH STATE

Exciting Entry

On this day in 1850, Patrick Floyd Garrett was born. Garret held several positions over his lifetime, including sheriff; but he is best remembered as the lawman who shot and killed "Billy the Kid."

Prominent Passing

On this day in 1875, Alexander Ramsey died. He was the sheriff of Ellis County, Kansas. While capturing a horse thief, a gunfight ensued and Ramsey was mortally wounded while the outlaw was killed.

Davy Crockett is a name known by most as a brave Tennessee frontiersman that died while valiantly fighting at the Alamo. However, he was actually born in a country that no longer exists and a state that never was accepted. Crockett was born in the Lost State of Franklin.

After the Revolutionary War, much of the land west of the Appalachian Mountains was never given a clear acceptance into the new country. Four counties in North Carolina, located in modern day Tennessee, decided to form their own state. They applied for statehood but were rejected by the Congress under the Article of Confederation.

They then decided to be an independent state and elected John Sevier as their president. Davy's father supported the new country that lasted from 1784 to 1789. Sevier would have Sevierville, Tennessee, named in his honor.

Davy Crockett was born in 1787, halfway through the country's brief existence. While the Lost State of Franklin failed, one thing did come from the attempt. The writers of the Constitution added a clause that no new state could be formed from an already existing state.

Crockett had a resurgence of popularity in the 1950s and 1960s when Walt Disney produced a mini-series on his life and his name was once again a household name. The mini-series also popularized David Crockett's shortened name, Davy, although he was called this in his lifetime.

June **6**

SAM HOUSTON: CENSURED BY CONGRESS

Sam Houston was the first president of Texas, the only American to serve as governor of two different states, and as a congressman. While a former congressman, Houston beat up Ohio Congressman William Stanbery.

While on the House floor, Stanbery had attacked Houston, suggesting that as governor of Tennessee, he defrauded the Cherokee Indians. Houston demanded an apology and even suggested a duel, but both were ignored.

Soon thereafter, Houston and Stanberry met while walking down Pennsylvania Avenue, and a fight broke out. Houston began to beat the smaller Stanbery with a hickory cane. In defense, Stanbery drew a gun, but it misfired. Houston then hit him several more times before walking off.

Congress ordered Houston to be arrested and tried before Congress. He had Francis Scott Key for his lawyer; however, Congress found Houston in contempt of Congress but was only reprimanded by the Speaker, as Houston had several powerful political friends.

Remarkable Remark
"Would it not have been strange that I should seek to dishonor my country through her representatives, when I have ever been found ready... to do and suffer in her service?"
—Houston's summation

Exciting Entry
On this day in 1862, Churchill Jones Bartlett was born. He became a justice of the peace in 1895 and later served in Texas's House of Representatives. He also served as the Texas secretary of state.

Prominent Passing
On this day in 1865, William Quantrill died. He led a guerrilla unit that fought for the South in the Civil War. His unit raided Lawrence, Kansas, in 1863, leaving over one hundred fifty people dead.

Still wanting Houston punished, Stanbery filed a criminal complaint in a local court that fined Houston $500. Houston never paid the fine, and Andrew Jackson, his mentor, pardoned him. Houston soon headed out West to Texas and eventually became the president of the Republic of Texas.

WHITMAN'S GREAT TREK

Remarkable Remark

"If the Board dismisses me, I will do what I can to save Oregon to the Country. My life is of but little worth if I can save this country to the American people."

—Marcus Whitman

Exciting Entry

On this day in 1850, Benjamin Cheever Jr. was born. He served in three wars, including many battles during the Indian Wars, and earned the Medal of Honor for his then-heroic actions against the Sioux.

Prominent Passing

On this day in 1866, Chief Seattle died. Chief Seattle successfully made peace with the settlers; and the city that the settlers founded, called Seattle, was named in honor of his willingness to make peace.

Marcus Whitman was an early pioneer, missionary, and doctor in the Oregon Country. He was aided by his wife Narcissa and their friends, Henry and Eliza Spalding.

Even though the missionaries worked tirelessly, they saw few converts, and the mission board decided to shut the mission down. Whitman, not wanting to close the mission and lose the Oregon Country to England, started a trip back East on horseback during the winter.

Many travelers would not risk this journey in good weather, yet Whitman's desire to keep his mission work alive drove him to bravely make the journey through the winter. He and few others trekked across the West through many snowstorms, icy rivers, and snowy paths.

On arriving in the East, Whitman went to Washington D.C., where Whitman met with President Tyler and Secretary of State Daniel Webster and discussed issues relating to Oregon. He then went to Boston to report to his mission board, which greeted him coldly for making an unrequested, dangerous trip. However, many viewed Whitman as the man who saved the Oregon Country for the United States and as a believer of America's Manifest Destiny.

On his return West, Whitman led one of the largest wagon trains that ever crossed America to Oregon Country. Whitman is remembered today for his brave journeys across the land and for his mission efforts in Oregon.

GERONIMO

Perhaps one of the most well-known and feared Indians in the West was Geronimo. After Mexicans destroyed his village and killed his family, Geronimo spent nearly the next twenty-five years attacking and running from the US troops.

He surrendered after a 3,000-mile chase and agreed to be exiled for two years before returning. However, he remained a prisoner for over two decades. Geronimo was a prisoner at Fort Pickens near Pensacola, Florida; Mount Vernon Barracks, Alabama; and Fort Sill, Oklahoma.

While still a prisoner, Geronimo was allowed to appear at the 1904 St. Louis World's Fair, sign autographs, and even perform in a Wild West show. Although perceived as an Indian chief by the public, Geronimo was never an Indian chief and became displeased whenever people called him one.

In 1905, Geronimo was given the opportunity to be in President Theodore Roosevelt's inaugural parade. Geronimo and five actual chiefs rode horses down Pennsylvania Avenue in an effort to show that the Indians and the white man were at peace once again.

Geronimo eventually met Roosevelt and appealed to be allowed to return to Arizona, but the meeting was cut short. Geronimo was later permitted to write an autobiography, which he dedicated to Teddy Roosevelt. He remained a prisoner until his death in 1909.

Remarkable Remark

"Because he has read that story [I have written] and knows I try to speak the truth… I dedicate this story of my life to Theodore Roosevelt, President of the United Sates."
—*Geronimo autobiography*

Exciting Entry

On this day in 1859, Frank Dalton was born. Dalton was considered one of the West's bravest lawman. His brothers were members of Dalton gang, but he died prior to his brothers' becoming outlaws.

Prominent Passing

On this day in 1892, Robert Newton Ford died. He was a member of Jesse James's gang and is best known for killing James after the Missouri governor secretly agreed to give Ford a pardon if he did so.

OHIO BECOMES A STATE

Exciting Entry

On this day in 1824, George Tobey Anthony was born. Anthony was the seventh governor of Kansas and served one term from 1877 to 1879. He sought for educational and criminal justice reform within Kansas.

Prominent Passing

On this day in 1904, Harvey "Kid Curry" Logan died. Logan took his own life after being heavily wounded; however, several unproven reports stated that he never died and made his way to South America.

When the Revolutionary War ended, the Ohio Territory was incorporated as part of the Northwest Territory. Supporters of Ohio statehood wanted it to become a state; but they did not have enough people living in the area.

However, a Congressional committee determined that Ohio had enough people in the territory, and a bill enabling Ohio to form a constitution and state government was signed into law in early 1802. In late 1802, the eastern portion of the Northwest Territory met to form a constitution and state government.

The Ohio constitution was adopted in November 1802 and was sent to Congress as qualification for statehood. In February 1803, Congress passed an act stating Ohio's adopted constitution was in accordance with their 1802 enabling act and declared federal law to be enforced in the new state of Ohio.

In 1952, Ohio was about to celebrate its 150th year of statehood, and historians went to get the documents that made Ohio a state. However, they couldn't find any. This happened because although Congress ordered federal law to be enforced, it never declared Ohio to be a state.

To fix the problem, a congressman decided to undertake a little legal time travel. A joint resolution was introduced that allowed Ohio to be a state in 1803, solving the problem. Ohio officially became a state in 1953, effective 150 years earlier.

CRAZY HORSE

Of the many Indians who fought against the US government for the right to keep their own land, few are as famous as Crazy Horse. Crazy Horse was a Lakota warrior, and his most well-known battle was at the Battle of the Little Bighorn.

In the 1940s, Lakota leaders wanted to honor this great man of the past. They hired sculptor Korczak Ziolkowski, who had worked on Mount Rushmore, to create a monument carved out of the Black Hills. Ziolkowski often worked alone or with a skeletal staff and worked on the project until his death in 1982, with the monument far from finished.

In an effort to keep the project a private endeavor, Ziolkowski refused millions in federal funding. His family continues to slowly build the memorial. Ruth, Ziolkowski's widow, took over the project until her death in 2014 and oversaw the finish of Crazy Horse's head, in an effort to get more tourists into the area. People can still visit the site, and ultimately, the monument will be several times larger than Mount Rushmore, and to some, of far greater significance.

Remarkable Remark
"When you [the Ziolkowski's] start making money rather than to try to complete the [Crazy Horse] project, that's when, to me, it's going off in the wrong direction."
—*Crazy Horse descendant*

Exciting Entry
On this day in 1839, Wilburn Hill King was born. King served in the Civil War, ran a sugar plantation in Central America, served in Texas state politics, and wrote the *History of the Texas Rangers*.

Prominent Passing
On this day in 1883, John Mitchell Merrill died. He served in the US Cavalry during the Indian Wars and earned the Medal of Honor in 1880 for his heroic service, even after being badly wounded.

Some relatives of Crazy Horse feel that the Ziolkowski family is taking their time sculpting to continue making money off the project. They also feel that creating a monument in hills viewed as sacred by the people the monument is made to honor is only insulting their own beliefs.

 June 11

BILLY THE KID

Exciting Entry
On this day in 1848, William Hall was born. He served in the US military primarily out West, served in several battles of the Indian Wars, and earned the Medal of Honor for his valiant service.

Prominent Passing
On this day in 1955, Rose Dunn died. The many notorious outlaws she knew in her early years gave her the nickname "Rose of Cimarron." She later became an upright citizen and the wife of a politician.

The West had its fair share of outlaws and gunslingers, yet one of the most famous outlaws never held up a train or bank and was best known for participating in a feud.

In 1878, the "Lincoln County War" was occurring out in frontier New Mexico when competitors John Tunstall versus James Dolan and Lawrence Murphy began threatening each other. Billy the Kid and some others were hired to protect Tunstall, while Dolan and Murphy, although in the wrong, had the sheriff's support. Soon after the killing of Tunstall, a major gunfight ensued, leaving the sheriff dead and Billy the Kid on the lam with a reputation as the West's best gunman.

Amazingly, the Kid was known mainly for killing the sheriff, and he never held up a bank, stagecoach, or train. He mainly rustled cattle and occasionally stole horses. However, he was involved in the deaths of nine men during his brief lifetime, and once after being sentenced to hang, he broke out of jail, killing two guards during his escape.

Billy the Kid, though a famous outlaw, only lived to be twenty-one before being shot to death by lawman Pat Garrett. However, some believe that Billy the Kid was never actually killed and lived to die a natural death. Regardless of how he died, the Kid has been immortalized in over four dozen movies and is one of the West's well-known outlaws.

June 12 — BASS REEVES

In 1838 in Arkansas, one of the United States' most legendary lawmen was born. Bass Reeves escaped slavery during the Civil War and became a freedman after the war was over. It was soon thereafter that Reeves became a US deputy marshal and carved his place in history.

Reeves stood at six feet two inches and was one of the few African Americans selected as a marshal. He was the first black US deputy marshal west of the Mississippi River. Reeves was known for his high moral standards and values and even arrested his own son after he was accused of murder.

Over his thirty-two years as a lawman, it is estimated that he arrested over three thousand people and killed fourteen outlaws without being wounded. Many times, Reeves utilized unique ways to capture the outlaws. He once faked being an outlaw to be accepted into the outlaw's home for the evening and arrested the real outlaws during the night.

Some historians also believe that Bass Reeves was the inspiration behind the fictional character the Lone Ranger. However, there is no verifiable evidence to prove that Reeves was the inspiration, but many of Reeves's real-life actions and experiences tend to fall in line with what the Lone Ranger experienced. Regardless of who inspired the Lone Ranger, Bass Reeves was one of the West's greatest lawman and etched his place in history.

Remarkable Remark

"We can, however, say unequivocally that Bass Reeves is the closest real person to resemble the fictional Lone Ranger on the American western frontier of the nineteenth century."
—Art T. Burton

Exciting Entry

On this day in 1840, Thomas "Bear River" Smith was born. Smith was the marshal in Abilene, Kansas, and was known for not carrying a gun, as he preferred using his fists to settle official matters.

Prominent Passing

On this day in 1980, Milburn Stone died. He is best remembered for his role as Doctor Adams in the popular show *Gunsmoke*. He was inducted into the Great Western Performers Hall of Fame posthumously.

TRANSCONTINENTAL RAILROAD

Remarkable Remark

"May God continue the unity of our Country as this Railroad unites the two great Oceans of the world. Presented by David Hewes San Francisco."
—*Engraved on the last spike which was made of gold*

Exciting Entry

On this day in 1834, John Strachan was born. He emigrated from Scotland and traveled out West before settling in Wisconsin. He was in the US Army and was elected to the Wisconsin state assembly.

Prominent Passing

On this day in 1905, Wilmot Brooking died. He settled in the Dakota Territory and lost his feet to frostbite soon thereafter. He served in Dakota Territory politics and had a city named after him.

Early in American history, traveling anywhere was typically a long journey, often spanning days. However, as modern inventions such as the railroad were introduced, traveling times were greatly shortened.

As families began moving West, the railroad often led the way or soon followed. In 1862, the Union Pacific and the Central Pacific railroads were tasked with building a railroad that would link the entire country. However, the ongoing Civil War slowed work greatly and it was not until 1869 that the two companies met.

The Union Pacific primarily used Civil War veterans and those of Irish descent, while the Central Pacific primarily used Chinese workers to build the railroad. In 1866, both companies began laying tracks which stretched for nearly two thousand miles. In 1869, they finished both ahead of schedule and under budget.

On May 10, 1869, the two railroads met at Promontory Summit, Utah, and transcontinental travel became possible. Many people incorrectly place this historic occasion at Promontory Point, Utah, but this wrong location most likely came about because many of the newspapers had written their stories on the meeting in advance and did not bother to correct their error. Regardless, speedy, efficient travel was now available to all Americans, and soon, many other transcontinental railroads were built.

 # US CAMEL CORPS

During the 1830s, the American West was beginning to be settled. In 1836, it was suggested the best way to deal with the arid western terrain was by importing camels.

In 1855, Jefferson Davis, the secretary of war, convinced the president and Congress to provide $30,000 for the experiment of importing camels out West.

The Navy provided a ship and rigged it to be able to hold camels. After nearly a year of travel, the crew, through purchase and gifts, obtained thirty-three animals: nineteen females and fourteen males. The voyage saw one camel die and six calves born with two surviving the trip. They arrived back in Texas in May of 1856.

Davis sent the ship back to purchase more camels while the current camels were tested in the American West. Several tests proved camels were a good alternative, and in 1857, forty-one more camels were brought to the United States.

Ironically, the only battle action the camels saw was under civilians, when Mohave Indians threatened the man holding the camels and he led a charge routing the Indians. The Civil War essentially ended the camel experiment, even though the new secretary of war wanted to purchase a thousand more camels. The camels were eventually sold and often ended up in circuses. The last camel from the original group supposedly died in 1934 at the age of eighty. The experiment was unofficially known as the US Camel Corps.

Remarkable Remark

"Sir: [You are] Assigned to special duty in connexion with the appropriation for 'importing camels for army transportation and for other military purposes'."
—*Orders from Davis for camel importation*

Exciting Entry

On this day in 1854, Nat "Deadeye Dick" Love was born. He was born a slave (his birthdate is not certain because of this) and was considered one of the best all-around cowhands during his lifetime.

Prominent Passing

On this day in 1914, D. L. "Billy Wilson" Anderson died. He joined Billy the Kid's gang and evaded the law for many years before moving to Texas. He gained a presidential pardon and became a lawman.

ELMER MCCURDY

Exciting Entry
On this day in 1836, George L. Shoup was born. He served as Idaho's first governor for roughly three months before he was elected as a senator to Congress for Idaho, the position he actually wanted.

Prominent Passing
On this day in 1937, Adelbert Cronkhite died. He served in many wars, including the Sioux Wars. He retired as a major general, and after his death, the United States renamed a fort in California after him.

In 1911, small-time outlaw Elmer McCurdy met his untimely demise after robbing a train (that he thought had thousands of dollars) of $46 and two jugs of whiskey. However, McCurdy is best remembered not for his time alive but for the time he was dead!

Following his death, the embalmer found no one willing to pay for his embalming; therefore, he propped McCurdy, filled with arsenic, in a display and charged people to visit him. Since he was becoming a popular attraction, disguised carnival workers claimed the body of McCurdy.

Over the next few decades, McCurdy appeared as a sideshow freak, an exhibit at the Los Angeles museum of crime, a prop in films, and as a glow-in-the-dark monster in a Long Beach amusement ride. It was not until December of 1976 that people realized that this prop dummy was actually a real person.

A worker with the show *The Six Million Dollar Man* was attempting to move McCurdy while at an onsite shoot at the amusement park, when the "prop's" arm fell off. It was then that the man realized there were bones in the prop. The grotesque discovery led to a search that determined the dead person was small-time outlaw Elmer McCurdy. Elmer McCurdy had poems, stories, and even television shows mentioned him after his discovery. It seemed that the fame he had sought in life was found only decades after his death.

WYATT EARP, BOXING

Many lawmen were considered good, honest men; however, there was the occasional lawman that could not decide which side of the law to be on. Wyatt Earp was a member of the latter group, being arrested numerous times for various deeds, but he tended to always remain unscathed and went back to his duties as a lawman.

After the shootout at OK Corral, for which he was arrested but later exonerated, Earp moved around the West, attempting to keep a low profile. Earp gambled, trained racehorses, and promoted prizefights to help make a living.

In 1896, Earp refereed a championship heavyweight boxing match and was soon the most infamous man in the West. Roughly ten thousand people gathered in San Francisco to watch the bout between Bob Fitzsimmons and Tom Sharkey. The match went into its eighth round when the dominate Fitzsimmons knocked Sharkey to the ground. Earp quickly called the punch illegal (which it was), disqualified Fitzsimmons, and gave the victory to Sharkey.

Exciting Entry
On this day in 1829, Geronimo was born. He was an Apache warrior who evaded permanent capture for many years. After his capture, he was held at Fort Pickens near Pensacola, Florida, for several years.

Prominent Passing
On this day in 1921, William "Bronco Bill" Walters died. He was an outlaw in the New Mexico area and was sentenced to life imprisonment. However, he was pardoned and died from falling off a windmill.

Many of the people in attendance believed that Earp fixed the fight, the main reason being that they all were betting on Fitzsimmons to win the fight, and they took the decision to court. Ultimately, Earp was fined only for illegally carrying a firearm, and the case was dropped, mainly because prizefighting was illegal. Decades later, people still called fixing fights "pulling an Earp."

JESSE JAMES

Remarkable Remark

"Jesse had a wife,
The joy of his life;
His children they were brave;
'Twas a thief and a coward
That shot Captain How-
ard [James' alias]
And laid…James in his grave."

Exciting Entry

On this day in 1859, Blu-
ford Duck was born. A
Cherokee outlaw, he
was sentenced to death
for killing two men. The
sentence was reduced
to life in prison, and he
was eventually par-
doned before he died.

Prominent Passing

On this day in 1887,
Benjamin F. Potts died.
Potts was the territorial
governor over Mon-
tana and served from
1870 to 1883. He was a
highly effective leader
and helped to expand
the territory's power.

Of all the West's many outlaws, perhaps the biggest name among them would be Jesse James. James made a name for himself by robbing and killing people. However, it was one of his own members that finally killed him, and not a lawman.

During and after the Civil War, James and his gang robbed several banks and trains. Because he sympathized with the South, he often left Southerners alone, while robbing those from the North. However, in 1876, a failed robbery of a Minnesota bank left the James gang either in prison or on the run.

Jesse James hid out in Tennessee under an assumed name and took up farming for several years. However, he soon went back to his old ways and formed another gang. Among the members of the gang were Charlie and Bob Ford.

Missouri governors had previously attempted to capture Jesse James and his gang, but the state's new governor, Thomas Crittenden, had a new plan. He decided to convince one of James's own gang to turn on him and kill him. That man was Bob Ford, who made a deal with the governor to kill James in exchange for a pardon and the reward money. On April 3, 1882, as Jesse James was moving into his new house, Bob Ford shot him in the back. Ironically, James was viewed as a hero and Bob Ford as the evil person. Many thought James was a Southern Robin Hood; however, most of what James did was for his own good and not for the good of others.

CARRY NATION

The West had many crazy characters, but none were as inciteful and passionate for a cause like Carry Nation.

Nation was a loud supporter of prohibition and often took measures to the extreme to stop the practice. Starting around 1890, she traveled through the Midwest lecturing on the evils of alcohol. She helped start a local chapter of the Woman's Christian Temperance Union (WCTU), and she and other women began singing and praying in front of bars.

However, as she moved from town to town, her tactics began to get more and more violent. She used anything she could get her hands on to help her in smashing a bar, including an umbrella, bricks, and a hatchet. It was this violence that gained her national attention and prompted the nickname Carry "Hatchet" Nation. She sold small souvenir hatchets for money and unsuccessfully tried to start small newspapers and magazines.

In 1903, Nation changed her name from "Carrie" to "Carry" to symbolize her carrying the nation toward prohibition. Her strong-arm tactics often ended in her being beaten or thrown in jail, but she often went right back to attacking bars. She once even intruded into the governor's chamber in Topeka. She also supported women's suffrage and attacked tobacco use. She published her autobiography a few years before she passed away in 1911.

Remarkable Remark
"I threw [the rocks] as hard, and as fast as I could, smashing mirrors and bottles and glasses and it was astonishing how quickly this was done.... God was certainly standing by me."
—*Carry A. Nation*

Exciting Entry
On this day in 1873, Charles Du Val Roberts was born. He was born on the Cheyenne Indian Agency where his father worked and served in the US Army for forty years, earning the Medal of Honor in Cuba.

Prominent Passing
On this day in 1920, Jewett William Adams died. Adams was the fourth governor of Nevada and served from 1883 to 1887. He helped expand the railroad and silver industries during his time in office.

PONY EXPRESS

Remarkable Remark

"I, [insert name], do hereby swear, be-fore the Great and Living God, that… I will… [not] use profane language… and that in every respect I will conduct myself honestly… So help me."
—*Rider's oath*

Exciting Entry

On this day in 1858, John Eugene Osborne was born. He served as governor of Wyoming from 1893 to 1895. He also served a term in Congress and as assistant secretary of state under Wilson from 1913 to 1917.

Prominent Passing

On this day in 1867, Henry Dodge died. He served as governor of the Wisconsin Territory from 1836 to 1841 and from 1845 to 1848. He also served in Congress and declined another territorial governorship.

In early 1860, the Central Overland California & Pike's Peak Express Company went into business. Better known as the Pony Express, it only lasted eighteen months before it went out of business.

As the nation expanded, the need for a fast, efficient mail system was needed. The Pony Express promised to deliver the mail from St. Joseph, Missouri, to Sacramento, California, in ten days. The journey was roughly 2,000 miles long, and each rider rode roughly 75–100 miles, stopping to switch horses every 10–15 miles, to accomplish this goal.

On average, each rider was twenty years old, weighed 100–125 pounds, and was expected to be willing to ride through possible danger. They also had to swear an oath of allegiance, be well familiarized with the territory, and able to ride though any weather. The riders were paid $100–$150 per month, while station keepers, who had the deadliest job, were typically paid around $50 a month.

On April 3, 1860, the first rider started with the mail, and exactly ten days later, the mail arrived in Sacramento. However, the business never was financially stable, and when the transcontinental telegraph line was completed, the Pony Express went virtually out of business. However, the Pony Express does modern day re-rides, allowing people to send letters across the West just like they would have done in the 1860s.

 **THE REAL WILD WEST**

The Wild West provides the perfect place for legends to be born. Cowboys, Indians, lawmen, and outlaws all came together either in peace or war to create the period known as the Wild West.

As towns began springing up beside the railroads, they offered new possibilities for those looking to start fresh. Ranchers with hundreds of heads of cattle and steer began to dot the West, and cattle drives to sell the meat back East began. The rise of cattlemen or cowboys led to dozens of cowboys making a name in history for themselves. However, contrary to what one sees on television, roughly one in every four cowboys was black, and typically was treated as an equal.

Prosperous towns, ranches, and farmers also led to the rise of two other groups— lawmen and outlaws. Outlaws often formed gangs and went from place to place attacking trains, stagecoaches, and banks; while lawmen chased the desperadoes across the West in an attempt to bring them to justice.

Indian tribes across the West felt that the influx of settlers was an invasion of the land they were promised by the US government. Unfortunately, the US government did not always treat the Indians fairly, and many Indian agents took advantage of the Indians, often leading to bloodshed. Ultimately, every person helped shape the West in his own way and helped to create the unique legendary status of this time period.

Remarkable Remark
"American history has been in a large degree the history of the colonization of the Great West.... The frontier is the line of most rapid and effective Americanization."
—*Frederick Jackson Turner*

Exciting Entry
On this day in 1844, Francis E. Warren was born. He served in many capacities including Wyoming's territorial senate, Wyoming's treasurer, mayor of Cheyenne, and governor of the Territory of Wyoming.

Prominent Passing
On this day in 1912, Daniel Keating died. Keating served as a corporal in the US military out West during the Indian Wars. He earned the Medal of Honor in 1870 for his valor during an Indian chase.

June 21

OK CORRAL

Remarkable Remark

"When... [they] drew their pistols; I knew it was a fight for life and I drew and fired in defense of my own life and the lives of my brothers and Doc Holliday."

—Wyatt Earp

Exciting Entry

On this day in 1842, George W. Littlefield was born. Littlefield became wealthy enough to retire before he was forty and donated over $300,000 to improve the University of Texas's archival material.

Prominent Passing

On this day in 1892, Lot Smith died. Smith, a Mormon, was an active leader in the conflict between the US government and the Mormon church. Navajos ambushed his settlement and shot him to death.

In the West, many outlaws and lawmen made their mark in history through a gunfight. Quite possibly, however, the most famous shootout in the American West was the gunfight behind the OK Corral.

In 1877, silver was found near Tombstone, Arizona, and the town soon became a profitable location. In the town, Wyatt Earp, a former lawman, served as a bank guard, while his brothers, Morgan and Virgil, were the area's marshals.

At a nearby ranch, the McLaurys and Clantons lived as cowboys but also rustled cattle and stole to keep the money coming in. The Clanton-McLaury gang wanted to control Tombstone and the county, and the power struggle between the gang and the Earps ended in a shootout.

In October 1881, the two opposing sides had several violent incidents, including members of the Clanton-McLaury gang getting pistol-whipped. On October 26, 1881, the feelings between the two factions erupted. Six members of the Clanton-McLaury gang were behind the OK Corral when the Earp brothers and their friend Doc Holliday went to confront them. In just thirty seconds, some thirty shots were fired, and the gunfight was over.

Three members of the Clanton-McLaury gang were killed, and Virgil and Morgan Earp along with Doc Holliday were wounded. The Earp's and Holliday were arrested for murder, but a judge later ruled them innocent. The thirty-second gunfight still remains the most prominent gunfight in America's history.

PINKERTON DETECTIVE AGENCY

In the 1850s, the Pinkerton Detective Agency, started by Allan Pinkerton, opened its doors and soon became the leader in detective and protective work.

By the 1870s, the Pinkertons had the world's largest criminal database, made up of thousands of mugshots, reports, and newspaper clippings. They were often hired to protect trains and stagecoaches and were often brought in after a robbery.

The Pinkertons also worked to disband several Western outlaws and stopped the Dalton gang, Reno gang, Molly McGuire gang, and Butch Cassidy's Wild Bunch. On one case, Pinkerton detectives chased a group of robbers to Canada, and after capturing them, recovered roughly $300,000 dollars.

However, the only gang it seemed unable to capture was the James-Younger gang. While chasing after Jesse James, a posse of Pinkerton men attacked his home, expecting Jesse and Frank James to be there. However, the James brothers had been tipped off and in the ensuing struggle at the James home, James's mother was wounded, and his eight-year-old half-brother was killed. The Pinkertons were suddenly looked at as villains themselves, and they slowly attempted to shift public favor back to them.

Following Chicago's Great Fire, Pinkerton guards were hired to protect the town from looting and later helped break up labor strikes. The Pinkertons are still in business today as a security company.

Remarkable Remark

"I suddenly found myself called upon, from every quarter, to undertake matters requiring the detective skill, until I was soon actually *forced* to [become a detective]."
—Allan Pinkerton

Exciting Entry

On this day in 1835, Cullen M. Baker was born. Baker was a desperado who killed many people, including numerous slaves merely, for being in his way. He was shot and killed by a school teacher.

Prominent Passing

On this day in 1839, Major Ridge died. He was a Cherokee leader that supported the peaceful removal of the Cherokees. He was assassinated by those who had opposed the Cherokee removal.

CHICAGO RAISED ITS CITY

Exciting Entry
On this day in 1842, Arthur Mellette was born. He was provisional governor of South Dakota and provisional governor of the Dakota Territory and supported Dakota farmers during a multi-year drought.

Prominent Passing
On this day in 1912, George Wratten died. He was an Indian interpreter for the US government. While free, he lived with Geronimo and his band of exiles after they were captured and imprisoned.

As Americans moved from the rural areas to cities during the mid-1800s, many cities out West began to grow. Chicago, built right along Lake Michigan, often found itself flooded, and sewage often filled the streets. As the town grew, this problem amplified until 1855, when the city began the process of raising the city.

Because the city was only a few feet above Lake Michigan, sewage wouldn't properly drain, and the Chicago Board of Sewerage Commissioners determined the best way to end the problem was to raise the entire city several feet.

In the roughly twenty years that Chicago was raised, city drainage pipes were installed, and dirt and new foundations were placed under buildings. Many businesses were raised inch by inch while still being open to visitors. Once, a part of a city block, weighing roughly 35,000 tons, was raised using 6,000 jackscrews and hundreds of men. This process was possible because modern skyscrapers and building materials like iron weren't commonly used and most buildings were heavy and well built. George Pullman was one of the masterminds behind the project and later made his fortune in building railroad sleeping cars. Today such a feat would be nearly impossible, yet in the late 1800s, Chicago raised its city higher to continue to grow, spurring the town to new growth during the turn of the century.

 June **24**

JOSEPHINE DOODY

Josephine Doody was born in 1853 in Georgia and left home for Colorado at a young age. It is assumed she went to Colorado with a man, but the relationship failed.

After she shot a man, supposedly in self-defense, Doody went on the run and ended up in a small town in Montana. It is assumed that during this time she developed her opioid addiction. She caught the eye of Dan Doody, who essentially kidnapped her and headed to his cabin along Flathead River.

During this time, she got sober, and shortly thereafter got married to Dan Doody. Dan was one of the first park rangers at Montana's Glacier National Park, but he lost his job in 1916 because of his poaching. With their cabin being located near the Great Northern Railroad, she saw an opportunity for business and began moonshining. She delivered her moonshine to the passing trains.

Josephine kept her moonshining business after Dan died in 1921. After she gave up moonshining, she became close friends with another park ranger named Clyde Fauley Sr. during the 1920s, and then with Charlie Holland in the 1930s. When Josephine became ill in 1936 with pneumonia, Holland sent her on a train to nearby Kalispell to receive treatment, though she protested. Once she arrived at the hospital, she lost consciousness and never regained it. She passed away at the age of eighty-two and was known as the "Bootleg Lady of Glacier Park."

Remarkable Remark
"Josephine developed a thriving bootleg operation... the train would stop at Doody siding, and each toot of the whistle would mean one gallon of moonshine."
—*John Fraley,*
Doody historian

Exciting Entry
On this day in 1800, Kintzing Pritchette was born. Pritchette was Oregon Territory's governor for sixty days until the new governor arrived. He was also the defense lawyer in the Whitman Massacre trial.

Prominent Passing
On this day in 2003, Alex Gordon died. He was a film producer who produced a few Western movies. He worked with his idol Gene Autry and wrote the documentary *Gene Autry, America's Singing Cowboy*.

INDIANS IN WESTWARD EXPANSION

June 25

When European settlers emigrated to the Americas, they were met by numerous indigenous tribes which themselves emigrated to the land. As settlers began moving West, however, many of these tribes were pushed out of their land.

Indian Wars were battles between these tribes and the colonies, and later the US government. King Philip's War, Black Hawk War, Seminole War, and many other wars determined who would retain control of the land, ultimately ending with the Indians as the losers.

In peace time and in battles, many Indians were making a name for themselves and becoming legends for their deeds. Indians like Squanto, Sacagawea, Crazy Horse, Will Rogers, Jim Thorpe, Geronimo, Tecumseh, Sitting Bull, Pocahontas, and many other Indians became household names.

Many important events also affected tribes across the nation. The Trail of Tears, the Battle of the Little Bighorn, and the Wounded Knee Massacre forced Indian tribes onto reservations. However, Indians were granted citizenship in 1924, and Charles Curtis became the first Indian US vice president in 1929.

While many prefer to call Indians "indigenous people," "Native Americans," or "American Indians," most do not mind being called Indians and would honestly prefer to be called by their tribal name. In the end, however, we are all Americans and should work together to make our nation great.

CALIFORNIA GOLDRUSH

In 1848, gold was discovered at Sutter's Mill in California, leading to the California Gold Rush and the coining of the term "forty-niners."

However, the California gold rush was not actually the first to occur in the United States. Around fifty years previously, gold had been discovered in North Carolina, leading thousands of treasure hunters to travel there and begin mining. The Charlotte Mint was even established to help process the large amounts of gold.

During the California gold rush, more money was made by merchants than by miners. Famous entrepreneurs such as John Studebaker, Henry Wells, William Fargo, and Levi Strauss all had their successful beginnings supported by the gold rush.

Prices were so far out of hand that plain water would fetch as much as one hundred dollars because of prospectors not being prepared for the long journey, whereas bacon was tossed to the side of the road and abandoned when travelers realized that too much had been stored. At the outset of the gold rush, reports of people mining thousands of dollars' worth of gold brought even more people to the area.

Ultimately, most "forty-niners" went broke and either returned home or stayed in the area and worked. The biggest result of the gold rush was that within a few years of its start, California had enough people to become a state, and it joined the Union as the thirty-first state.

Remarkable Remark

"I have left those that I love as my own life behind & risked every thing and endured many hardships to get here, & I want to make enough to live easier & do some good [to others]."
—*Sheldon Shufelt*

Exciting Entry

On this day in 1842, Frank Baldwin was born. He is one of the few Americans who earned the Medal of Honor twice. His first was earned in the Civil War and his second in Texas during the Indian Wars.

Prominent Passing

On this day in 1927, June Mathis died. Mathis was from Colorado and was well known in the film industry. She worked on *Ben Hur: A Tale of the Christ* and helped launch Rudolph Valentino's career.

June 27

DALLAS STOUDENMIRE

Remarkable Remark

"We the undersigned parties…hereby agree that we will hereafter meet and pass each other on friendly terms, and that bygones shall be bygones."
—*Signed by Stoudenmire and the Manning brothers*

Exciting Entry

On this day in 1833, José Francisco Chaves was born. Chaves serves as New Mexico's territorial delegate to Congress for three terms from 1865 to 1871. He lobbied for the territory to become a state.

Prominent Passing

On this day in 1927, Moses Harris died. He earned the Medal of Honor in the Civil War and served out West after the Civil War. He was also Yellowstone National Park's first military superintendent.

Dallas Stoudenmire is a name few people remember today; however, during his lifetime, he was well known as a lawman and a gunfighter.

Stoudenmire was born in Alabama and served in the Confederate Army. Following the Civil War, he moved to Texas, where he supposedly killed several men. He later served in the Texas Rangers and then as a marshal in New Mexico.

In 1881, he moved to El Paso and was appointed the town's marshal soon after he arrived. El Paso was considered a violent town, and Stoudenmire, with his vicious temper and deadly accuracy, fit the bill for the town's new marshal.

It was in El Paso that Stoudenmire participated in the "Four Dead in Five Seconds" gunfight. When a rancher killed a local constable, Stoudenmire shot and killed the rancher and two other bystanders, including a former city marshal. Within a week, Stoudenmire killed another former city marshal after the city marshal attempted to assassinate Stoudenmire.

Stoudenmire left the area and got married, but soon returned to El Paso. Once back, a feud between Stoudenmire and another man became so problematic that the town forced the two sides to sign a peace treaty. Stoudenmire went on to become a US deputy marshal but was killed within the year. Stoudenmire helped clean up the streets of El Paso and became a legend in his own right.

June 28 — DALTON GANG

The West seemed to be a breeding ground for gangs and outlaws, and it was a never-ending fight between outlaws and lawmen. One of the most notorious gangs was the Dalton gang.

The oldest Dalton brother actually served as a deputy marshal and was never a part of the gang. However, two other brothers that were lawmen soon switched sides and formed a gang.

Members included Dick Broadwell, Bitter Creek Newcomb, Bill Power, Black-Faced Charlie, Bill Doolin, and four Dalton brothers. The gang often robbed trains and once made off with $17,000 dollars. They were also responsible for numerous deaths of lawmen and citizens that attempted to intercede in the robberies.

In 1892, five members of the Dalton gang rode into Coffeyville, Kansas, with the goal of pulling off a double bank robbery. However, the citizens of Coffeyville fought back, and four of the gang members were killed, as well as four townspeople. Amazingly, one of the gang members, Emmett Dalton, who had roughly twenty bullets in his body, survived and was sentenced to life in prison.

He was pardoned in 1907 and wrote a book about his time in the Dalton gang. He even returned to Coffeyville as a celebrity. However, several members of the original Dalton gang continued to terrorize the West, either in new gangs or by themselves.

Remarkable Remark

"At this critical juncture the citizens opened fire from the outside [of the bank] and the shots from their… [guns] pierced the plate-glass windows and rattled through the bank."
—David Elliott

Exciting Entry

On this day in 1857, Emerson Hough was born. He was a writer and was deeply intrigued with the frontier and the West. He wrote prolifically on places, people, and experiences throughout the West.

Prominent Passing

On this day in 1880, John "Texas Jack" Omohundro died. He was a scout, performer, and newspaper writer that performed with "Buffalo Bill" Cody and "Wild Bill" Hitchcock in their Wild West shows.

ANNIE OAKLEY

In 1860, Phoebe Ann Moses was born. Known as Annie Oakley, she was known world wide for her skill as a sharpshooter, and she married a sharpshooter whom she had beaten in a contest.

Oakley began shooting at an early age, and she considered one of her best shots to be one she made at the age of eight. She became famous while performing with Buffalo Bill's Wild West Show. Sitting Bull became close friends with Oakley and adopted her as his daughter, giving her the nickname "Little Sure Shot."

Her fame, however, often brought problems, and she sued William Randolph Hearst's newspaper over a libelous claim that she was a thief and a drug addict. Of the fifty-five libel suits Oakley brought against newspapers, she won or settled fifty-four suits, and Hearst himself had to pay her over $27,000. She performed at Wimbledon at a shooting competition and continued to grow her reputation as one of the best shots in the world.

Remarkable Remark
"The old man [Sitting Bull] was so pleased with me, he insisted upon adopting me, and I was then and there christened 'Watanya Cicilla,' or 'Little Sure Shot.'"
—*Annie Oakley*

Exciting Entry
On this day in 1834, Abel "Shanghai" Pierce was born. He was a powerful, wealthy cattleman who was known across the United States. He had a nearly thirty-foot statue created of him, and it became his grave marker.

Prominent Passing
On this day in 1894, Martin M'Rose died. He was a thief the jail released by accident. He was killed by a posse trying to arrest him, but some uncertainty remains if it was truly an accident.

Interestingly, Oakley's lasting legacy is in her name. When people went to circuses or sporting events, free tickets were often punched with holes to determine who actually paid. These pock-marked tickets often resembled playing cards that Oakley would shoot, and soon free tickets were referred to as "Annie Oakleys." In baseball, the term referred to a walk because it was a free pass to first base.

LAURA INGALLS WILDER

Laura Ingalls Wilder was born in 1867 in Wisconsin, and died in 1957 in Missouri. Known for her books, Wilder saw the explosion of travel in her lifetime.

As a young girl, she and her family traveled by covered wagon to Minnesota, Kansas, Iowa, Missouri, Indian Territory, and the Dakota Territory. When she was born, transcontinental travel by train was just coming about, and many still used wagons to move. However, as train travel became cheaper, she utilized it to settle in a new town.

In 1908, the Model T came into existence, and its cheap cost soon made travel by car accessible to all. Laura Ingalls Wilder, who lived much of her life in Missouri, took the family car for long drives to get off their farm. The modernization of airplanes and their more frequent use for public air travel allowed Laura Ingalls to take an airplane ride to California to visit her daughter and to view the Pacific Ocean.

Laura Ingalls Wilder's *Little House* book series were not published until she was in her sixties, and her daughter, Rose, helped her. Her books have been read by people everywhere. Her life travels exemplify the unique and rapid growth of transportation. From traveling weeks in a wagon as a young girl to flying across the country in a few short hours, she was one of many to experience the growth of America to new frontiers and the end of the Wild West.

Remarkable Remark
"I realized that I had seen and lived it all—all the successive phases of the frontier... I represented a whole period of American history."
—*Laura Ingalls Wilder*

Exciting Entry
On this day in 1853, Tom McLaury was born. McLaury was a cattleman and supposedly a notorious outlaw who was killed at the shootout at OK Corral. He was unarmed and murdered by Doc Holliday.

Prominent Passing
On this day in 1893, Frank Jones died. A Texas Ranger, he died while trying to capture cattle rustlers in a gunfight that occurred in Mexican territory. He was later returned to the states for burial.

CITATIONS

In the interest of historical accuracy, all quotes are from primary (or as closely as possible) sources and all quotes are seen exactly as from those sources. Citations provide the source of the quote and reveal who said the quote, the source (and author if different than the speaker), and publication information.

JANUARY

1. "Remarks at the 31st Annual Meeting of the Southern Legislative Conference." July 21, 1977 found in *Public Papers of the Presidents of the United States Jimmy Carter 1977* (Washington: United States Government Printing Office, 1978)
2. Preamble of the Charter of the United Nations and Statute of the International Court of Justice (San Francisco, 1945)
3. Bernard Baruch, address at the unveiling of his portrait in the South Carolina legislature, Columbia, South Carolina, April 16, 1947.—*Journal of the House of Representatives of the First Session of the 87th General Assembly of the State of South Carolina*, p. 1085. Found in *Respectfully Quoted: A Dictionary of Quotations* (New York: Barnes and Noble, 1993)
4. George F. Kennan, *Memoirs, 1950- 1963*, Volume 2 (Boston: Little, Brown, 1972)
5. NATO treaty, Article One
6. Winston Churchill, "Extract from Churchill's notes for the Iron Curtain speech" Reference: Church 5/4A from The Sir Winston Churchill Archive Trust
7. "Soviet Jokes for the DDCI" declassified in 2013 by the CIA FOIA: CIA-RDP89G00720R000800040003-6 (includes the three other jokes)
8. 4 U.S. Code § 4. Pledge of allegiance to the flag; manner of delivery
9. Douglas MacArthur, speech given in Congress on Thursday, April 19, 1951, quoted in *Proceedings of Congress and General Congressional Publications, Volume 97, Part 3 (March 27, 1951 to April 25, 1951) 82nd Congress, 1st Session* 4123 (Washington, D.C.: United States Government Publishing Office, 1951).
10. Arthur Summerfield, "Q and A with Summerfield on February 16, 1959" From the *Congressional Record: Proceedings and Debates of the 86th Congress First Session Volulme 105—Part 5*
11. Fidel Castro "Question and Answer with Fidel Castro" from CubaINFO Vol. 6 No. 1 (Cuban Studies Program at Johns Hopkins University, 1993)
12. Nikita Khrushchev, "Don't Play With Fire, Gentlemen" From the Concluding Words of Comrade N. S. Khrushchev to the Fifth Session of the Supreme Soviet USSR, Fifth Convocation on 7 May 1960 within the CIA report "Soviet Version of the U-2 Incident" FOIA: CIA-RDP80T00246A074400420001-9
13. John F. Kennedy, *With Kennedy* by Pierre Salinger (New York: Doubleday, 1966)
14. Author interview with Michala Archut
15. 1.Mikhail Gorbachev , American Jewish Historical Society Presents "Beyond the Pale: A Reunion Between President Mikhail Gorbachev and Secretary of State George Shultz moderated by Charlie Rose for the 2009 Emma Lazarus Statue of Liberty Award Luncheon at the Rainbow Room, March 26, 2009. Part 2 of 3."
16. Abba Eban, "Statement to the Security Council by Foreign Minister Eban- 6 June 1967" from *Israel's Foreign Relations Vols 1-2: 1947-1974*
17. Authorized King James Version and the Apollo 8 transcript
18. J.M. Boorda, "Statement of Vice Adm. J.M. Boorda, United States Navy, Deputy Chief of Naval Operations for Manpower, Personnel, and Training and Chief of Navy Personnel, Department of the Navy; Accompanied by Capt. Tom Kelly, Legislative Assistant, Department of the Navy" found in *U.S.S. Pueblo: Hearing Before the Investigations Subcommittee of the Committee on Armed Services, House of Representatives, One Hundred First Congress, First Session, Hearing Held June 23, 1989, Volume 4* (Washington D.C.: U.S. Government Printing Office, 1959)
19. Neil Armstrong, "Apollo 11 Technical Air-To-Ground- Voice Transcription (GOSS NET 1)" (Houston, 1969)
20. Richard Nixon "Address to the Nation on the War in Vietnam" November 3, 1969 found in *Public Papers of the Presidents of the United States Richard Nixon 1969* (Washington: United States Government Printing Office, 1971)

21. Briefing Officer, "Extension of Remarks *Crisis in Credibility* Hon. Edward J. Derwinski of Illinois in the House of Representatives" Tuesday, April 2, 1968 found in *Congressional Record: Proceedings and Debates of the 90th Congress Second Session* 8735
22. Roger Kimball, *The Long March* (San Francisco: Encounter Books, 2001)
23. Ezer Weizman, *The Battle for Peace* (Toronto: Bantam Books, 1981)
24. Jimmy Carter, "Interview With the President" Remarks and a Question-and-Answer Session With Editors and News Directors. April 6, 1979 found in *Public Papers of the Presidents of the United States Jimmy Carter 1979* (Washington: United States Government Printing Office, 1980)
25. Jimmy Carter, "Venice Economic Summit Conference" Exchange With Reporters Following the First Two Sessions. June 22, 1980 found in *Public Papers of the Presidents of the United States Jimmy Carter 1980-81* (Washington: United States Government Printing Office, 1982)
26. Jimmy Carter, "The President's News Conference" of November 30, 1978 found in *Public Papers of the Presidents of the United States Jimmy Carter 1978* (Washington: United States Government Printing Office, 1979)
27. Ronald Reagan, "Soviet joke" on August 11, 1984 from BBC's Witness History
28. Caspar Weinberger, "Remarks prepared for delivery by Secretary of Defense Caspar W. Weinberger to the Navy League of the United States, Washington, D.C., April 16, 1987. Found in the article "Openness: Theirs and Ours" *Defense Issues* Vol. 2 No. 27
29. George H. W. Bush, "Remarks at the Yale University Commencement Ceremony in New Haven, Connecticut" May 27, 1991 found in *Public Papers of the Presidents of the United States George Bush 1991* (Washington: United States Government Printing Office, 1992)
30. Ronald Reagan, "Remarks at the National Space Club Luncheon" March 29, 1985 found in *Public Papers of the Presidents of the United States Ronald Reagan 1985* (Washington: United States Government Printing Office, 1988)
31. Ronald Reagan, "Remarks on East-West Relations at the Brandenburg Gate in West Berlin" June 12, 1987 found in *Public Papers of the Presidents of the United States Ronald Reagan 1987* (Washington: United States Government Printing Office, 1989)

FEBRUARY
1. Phyllis Wheatley, "On Being Brought from AFRICA to AMERICA" from *Poems on Various Subjects, Religious and Moral* (London: A. Bell, 1773)
2. Richard Allen, *The Life, Experience, and Gospel Labors of the Rt. Rev. Richard Allen* (Philadelphia: F. Ford and M.A. Ripley, 1880)
3. John Minto, "Reminiscences of Experiences on the Oregon Trail In 1844.--II" from *The Quarterly of the Oregon Historical Society* Volume II Number 3 (September 1901)
4. Sojourner Truth, "Ain't I a Woman" speech given at a Women's Rights Convention in Akron, Ohio, on May 29, 1851, published in the Salem *Anti-Slavery Bugle* June 21, 1851
5. John Stauffer, "'Father of Black Nationalism' relegated to history's shadows" from the Toledo *Blade* February 5, 2011
6. *The Commonwealth vs. Nat Turner* found in *The Confessions of Nat Turner* (Baltimore: Thomas R. Gray, 1831)
7. Frederick Douglass "Speech at the National Free Soil Convention" August 11, 1852 found in *The Yale Book of Quotations* (Yale University Press, 2006)
8. Harriet Tubman at a Suffrage Convention in 1896 quoted in *The Yale Book of Quotations* (Yale University Press, 2006)
9. Robert Smalls, *Journal of the Constitutional Convention of the State of South Carolina* (Columbia, S.C.: Charles A. Calvo, Jr., 1895)
10. George Washington Buckner, "A Slave, Ambassador and City Doctor" found in *Indiana Slave Narratives* (Native American Book Publishers, 1938)
11. "SERIES OF FIERCE COMBATS Angered Whites Surround Negro Quarter and Set It on Fire." The New York *Times*, June 2, 1921
12. Inscription on George Washington Carver's grave
13. W.E.B. DuBois, "Address of the Niagara Movement, to the Country" found in *The Public* Vol. IX Number 439 (Chicago, Saturday, September 1, 1906)

14. Scott Joplin, "Exercise No. 1" from *School of Ragtime* (1908)
15. James Weldon Johnson, "Lift Every Voice and Sing" or the "National Hymn for the Colored People of America" from the *Lutheran Woman's Work* Vol. XII No. 3 (March, 1919)
16. Psalm 23: 4 Authorized King James Version
17. Benjamin Booker, "Benjamin Booker on Opening for Jack White" The New York *Times*, August 17, 2014
18. William Clinton, "Remarks Honoring General Benjamin O. Davis, Jr., of the Tuskegee Airmen" December 9, 1998 found in *Public Papers of the Presidents of the United States William J. Clinton 1998* (Washington: United States Government Printing Office, 2000)
19. P.G. Wodehouse, quoted in "Portrait of a cartoonist" by Bill Savage in the Chicago *Tribune* (2016)
20. Selma Burke, "Sculptor, 93, Carving Artworks, Opinions" by Steven Litt found in "A Special Salute to Dr. Selma Burke" from the *Congressional Record* Volume 140, Number 150 (Tuesday, December 20, 1994)
21. Bessie Coleman, quote from the Smithsonian National Air and Space Museum website
22. Martin Luther King, Jr., "Letter from a Birmingham Jail" (Birmingham, April 16, 1963)
23. Louis Armstrong, "Sayings of the Decade" London *Observer* December 28, 1969
24. Thurgood Marshall, "Marshall Urges Blacks to Press Equality Battle" The Los Angeles *Times* August 11, 1988
25. Jesse Owens, *The Sports 100* by Brad Herzog (Macmillan, 1995)
26. Lincoln, Abraham. *Abraham Lincoln papers: Series 2. General Correspondence. 1858 to 1864: Abraham Lincoln to Horace Greeley, Friday, Clipping from Aug. 23, 1862 Daily National Intelligencer, Washington, D.C.* 1862. Manuscript/Mixed Material. https://www.loc.gov/item/mal4233400/.
27. Shirley Chisholm, *Unbought and Unbossed* (New York: Avon Books, 1971)
28. Marian Anderson, *My Lord, What a Morning* (New York: Viking Press, 1956)
29. Edward W. Brooke, *Bridging the Divide: My Life* (New Brunswick, NJ: Rutgers University Press, 2007)

MARCH

1. Gay Robins "The Names of Hatshepsut as King" in *Egyptian Archaeology* Vol. 85 (1999), pp. 103-112 DOI: 10.2307/3822429
2. Joann Fletcher, "Who was Cleopatra?" by Amy Crawford Smithsonian.com March 31, 2007
3. Authorized King James Version
4. Empress Theodora, *Procopius* Vol. I, trans. by H. B. Dewing (London: William Heinemann, 1914)
5. Joan of Arc, *History of France* by Émile de Bonnechose trans. by William Robson (London: George Routledge, 1853)
6. Awestruck visitor, *Isabella of Castile: Europe's First Great Queen* by Giles Tremlett (Bloomsbury, 2017) citing an earlier untranslated Spanish book
7. Queen Elizabeth, "The Authentick Speech of Queen Elizabeth, to her Army encamp'd at Tilbury..." found in *The London Magazine: and Monthly Chronologer* (London: C. Acker, 1737)
8. Fred P. Wright, "Dr. Mary E. Walker" paper given before Oswego County Historical Society on May 19, 1953 found in Box 9, folder "Walker, Dr. Mary – Congressional - Medal of Honor, 1974 – 77" of the Bobbie Greene Kilberg Files, 1974 – 77 at the Gerald R. Ford Presidential Library
9. Herbert Hoover, "Address Accepting the Nomination" August 11, 1928 found in *Public Papers of the Presidents of the United States Herbert Hoover 1929* (Washington: United States Government Printing Office, 1974)
10. Smith, John, and Jay I. Kislak Reference Collection. *The generall historie of Virginia, New England & the Summer Isles: together with The true travels, adventures and observations, and A sea grammar.* Glasgow: J. MacLehose ; New York: Macmillan, 1907. Pdf. https://www.loc.gov/item/75320262/.
11. Sir Henry Sidney, "Sir Henry Sidney to Sir Francis Walsingham" March 1, 1583 Vol. 601, p. 89 found in *Calendar of the Carew Manuscripts* ed. by J. S. Brewer and William Bullen (London: Longmans, Green, Reader, Dyer, 1868)

12. Carl Gauss, *Carl Friedrich Gauss: Titan of Science* by G. Waldo Dunnington (New York: Exposition Press, 1955)
13. Bridget Bishop, "Examination of Bridget Bishop No. 1" from *Records of Salem Witchcraft* Vol. I (Roxbury, MA: privately printed for W. Elliot Woodward, 1864)
14. Patricia Krider, "Remembering the Ladies" by Amy Crawford Smithsonian.com February 1, 2007
15. Marie Antoinette, *Women of Beauty and Heroism* by Frank Goodrich (New York: Derby, Jackson, 1859) There are some other variations of this quote, but this is the earliest of accessible quotes
16. Susan Anthony, "The Status of Woman, Past, Present, and Future" found in *The Phonographic Magazine* Vol. XII No. 3 whole number 195 (Cincinnati, March, 1898)
17. Florence Nightingale, "Miss Nightingale to Miss H. Bonham Carter" 1861 found in *The Life of Florence Nightingale* by Sir Edward Cook Vol. I (London: Macmillan, 1913)
18. Louisa May Alcott, *An Old-Fashioned Girl* (Boston: Roberts Brothers, 1870)
19. Pierre Curie, "Radioactive substances, especially radium" Nobel Lecture June 6, 1905
20. Winston Churchill, *Great Contemporaries* (London: Butler, Tanner, 1939)
21. Helen Keller, *Optimism: An Essay* (New York: T.Y. Crowell, 1903)
22. Henry G. Wales, "Death Comes to Mata Hari" originally published in the *International News Service*, October 19, 1917 found in *Dispatches from the Front* by Nathaniel Lande (Oxford University Press, 1998)
23. Amelia Earhart, "Letter, 1937, to George Palmer Putnam" from the George Palmer Putnam Collection of Amelia Earhart Papers at Purdue University (1937)
24. Mother Teresa, obituary in the *Independent* September 6, 1997 quoted in *The Oxford Dictionary of Quotations* ed. by Elizabeth Knowles (Oxford university Press, 1999)
25. Jim Elliot, "October 28, 1949" from Jim Elliot's journal located at the Billy Graham Center, Wheaton, Illinois, Papers of Philip James Elliot- Collection 277
26. Hedy Lamarr, *Ecstasy and Me: My Life as a Woman* (New York: Bartholomew House, 1966)
27. Kalpana Chawla, "Columbia Accident Investigation Board Report Excepts" January 29, 2013 by SPACE.com Staff including "In Their Own Words… Remembering Columbia's Crew" SPACE.com Exclusive video
28. Margaret Thatcher, "Press Conference after winning Conservative leadership (Conservative Central Office)" February 11, 1975 from the BBC Sound Archive: OUP transcript
29. Barack Obama, "Computer Science Legend, Rear Adm. Grace Hopper, Posthumously Receives Presidential Medal of Freedom" November 11, 2016 by April Grant, Story Number: NNS161122-19 https://www.navy.mil/submit/display.asp?story_id=97807
30. Barbara Jordan, "Statement of Hon. Barbara Jordan…" found in *Debate on Articles of Impeachment* (Washington: U.S, Government Printing Office, 1974)
31. Madeleine Albright, "Madeleine Albright: An Exclusive Interview" by Marianne Schnall June 15, 2010 originally posted to the *HuffPost* Contributor platform.

APRIL
1. Preston Brooks, *Washington University Studies* Vol. VI No. 2 Humanistic Series (St. Louis: April, 1919)
2. Abraham Lincoln, "Speech April 10, 1865" found in *Collected Works of Abraham Lincoln* Vol. 8 from the *Collected works. The Abraham Lincoln Association, Springfield, Illinois. Roy P. Basler, editor; Marion Dolores Pratt and Lloyd A. Dunlap, assistant editors*. Lincoln, Abraham, 1809-1865. New Brunswick, N.J: Rutgers University Press, 1953.
3. Abraham Lincoln, "Letter to the King of Siam" February 3, 1862 found in *Collected Works of Abraham Lincoln* Vol. 5 from the *Collected works. The Abraham Lincoln Association, Springfield, Illinois. Roy P. Basler, editor; Marion Dolores Pratt and Lloyd A. Dunlap, assistant editors*. Lincoln, Abraham, 1809-1865. New Brunswick, N.J: Rutgers University Press, 1953.
4. Alfred Bellard, *Gone for a Soldier: The Civil War Memoirs of Private Alfred Bellard* (Boston: Little, Brown, 1975)
5. Belle Boyd, *Belle Boyd in Camp and Prison* (New York: Blelock, 1865)
6. Abraham Lincoln, "Speech to the One Hundred Sixty-Fourth Ohio Regiment" August 18, 1864 found in *Collected Works of Abraham Lincoln* Vol. 7 from the *Collected works. The*

Abraham Lincoln Association, Springfield, Illinois. Roy P. Basler, editor; Marion Dolores Pratt and Lloyd A. Dunlap, assistant editors. Lincoln, Abraham, 1809-1865. New Brunswick, N.J: Rutgers University Press, 1953.

7. Anonymous, *Lincoln President-Elect: Abraham Lincoln and the Great Secession Winter 1860-1861* by Harold Holzer (New York: Simon, Schuster, 2008) citing a letter found at the Library of Congress and Lincoln, Abraham. *Abraham Lincoln papers: Series 1. General Correspondence. 1833 to 1916: Anonymous. "A Citizen" to Abraham Lincoln, Thursday,Telegram reporting Lincoln was hanged in effigy.* November 8, 1860. Manuscript/ Mixed Material. https://www.loc.gov/item/mal0435600/. [Pensacola telegram]

8. Walt Whitman, "Patent-Office Hospital" 2 leaves handwritten. Early manuscript draft of an article printed in the New York Times found at the University of Virginia: Papers of Walt Whitman, Clifton Waller Barrett Library of American Literature, Albert H. Small Special Collections Library Box 1 Folder 45

9. Wilkinson, Dole, Nicolay, "Letter to Abraham Lincoln' August 27, 1862 from *Minnesota in the Civil and Indian Wars 1861-1865* Vol. II (St. Paul: Pioneer Press, 1893) [original in the Library of Congress]

10. Henry Stanley, *The Autobiography of Sir Henry Morton Stanley* ed. by Dorothy Stanley (Boston: Houghton Mifflin, 1909)

11. Abraham Lincoln, "A Letter from the President " August 22, 1862 from the New York *Tribune* Aug. 23, 1862. Abraham Lincoln to Horace Greeley

12. John Cockerill, "A Boy at Shiloh" found in *Under Both Flags* by Civil War veterans (Richmond: B. F. Johnson, 1896)

13. Abraham Lincoln, "Lincoln and the Jews" by Isaac Markens found in *Publications of the American Jewish Historical Society* Number 17 (Baltimore: Published by the Society, 1909)

14. Abraham Lincoln, "The Presidents Speech" found in *The Prairie Farmer* Vol. 10 No. 14 (Chicago: Published Saturday, October 4, 1862)

15. Nina Archibald, *Colors of Valor* by Patrick M. Hill (Minnesota Historical Society, Summer 2000)

16. Mary Ann Loughborough, *My Cave Life in Vicksburg* (New York: D. Appleton, 1864)

17. Abel Comstock, *History of the 21st Regiment Ohio Volunteer Infantry* by Captain S. S. Canfield (Toledo, OH: Vrooman, Anderson, Bateman, 1893)

18. E. P. Alexander, "The Great Charge and Artillery Fighting at Gettysburg" found in *Battles and Leaders of the Civil War* Vol. III (New York: The Century Company, 1888)

19. Veteran's account, *Recollections of a Private Soldier in the Army of the Potomac* by Frank Wilkeson (New York: G. P. Putnam's Sons, 1887)

20. J. L. Camp, "Letter from Camp to Author" found in *The Elmira Prison Camp* by Clay Holmes (New York: G. P. Putnam's Sons, 1912)

21. John Summerfield Staples, "Volunteer Enlistment" No. 39 signed October 1, 1864 (National Archives)

22. Bennett Young, *Daredevils of the Confederate Army* by Oscar A. Kinchen (Boston: Christopher Publishing, 1959)

23. Ely Parker, *The Life of General Ely S. Parker* by Arthur C. Parker (Buffalo, NY: Buffalo Historical Society, 1919)

24. Allen Pinkerton, *The Hour of Peril* by Daniel Stashower (New York: Minotaur Books, 2013)

25. J. W. Jones, *Christ in the Camp* (Richmond: B. F. Johnson, 1887)

26. *Shenandoah* ships log, "Ships log August 2, 1865" found in *Southern Historical Society Papers* Volume XXXII ed. by R. A. Brock (Richmond, VA: Published by the society, 1904)

27. James McPherson, "Historian revises estimate of Civil War dead" by Rachel Coker September 21, 2011 from Binghamton University https://discovere.binghamton.edu/news/ civilwar-3826.html

28. James Garfield, "Speech given in the House January 13, 1865" found in *The Congressional Globe* 38th Congress, 2d session (Washington D.C.: F. & J. Rives, Tuesday, January 17, 1865)

29. Montgomery Meigs, "Meigs to Edwin Stanton June 15, 1864" found in *On Hallowed Ground* by Robert M. Poole (New York: Bloomsbury, 2010)

30. E. B. Davis, "Letter in reply to Mr. Wayman A. Holland" found in "Gettysburg Monument Series- The Horse Hoof Question: An Enduring Myth from *The Blog of Gettysburg National Military Park* (posted July 20, 2012) https://npsgnmp.wordpress.com/2012/07/20/gettysburg-monument-series-the-horse-hoof-question-an-enduring-myth/

MAY

1. United States, United States Continental Congress, and American Imprint Collection. *Articles of confederation and perpetual union between the states of New-Hampshire, Massachusetts-Bay, Rhode-Island and Providence plantations, Connecticut, New-York, New-Jersey, Pennsylvania, Delaware, Maryland, Virginia, North-Carolina, South-Carolina and Georgia.* Lancaster, Pennsylvania printed ; Boston: Re-printed by John Gill, printer to the General Assembly, 1777. Online Text. https://www.loc.gov/item/11034113/. ["s" standardized throughout]
2. James Buchanan, "Monument to Washington" Thursday, January 15, 1824 found in *Proceedings and Debates of the House of Representatives of the United States*, 18th Congress 1st session 1045
3. John Adams, Letter from John Adams to Abigail Adams, 2 November 1800 [electronic edition]. *Adams Family Papers: An Electronic Archive.* Massachusetts Historical Society. http://www.masshist.org/digitaladams/
4. *Thomas Jefferson to Samuel H. Smith.* -09-21, 1814. Manuscript/Mixed Material. https://www.loc.gov/item/mtjbib021843/.
5. William Plumer, "Excerpt from William Plumer Papers (Library of Congress)" found in *History of American Presidential Elections* Volume I edited by Arthur Schlesinger (Philadelphia: Chelsea House, 2002)
6. James Parton, *Life of Andrew Jackson* Vol. I (New York: Mason Brothers, 1859)
7. "Turn Out! To the Rescue!" found in *The Harrison Medal Minstrel* (Philadelphia: Grigg, Elliott, 1840)
8. Thomas Miller, "The Case of the Late William Henry Harrison, President of the United States" found in The *Medical Examiner* Vol. IV No. 20 (Philadelphia, Saturday, May 15, 1841)
9. Harrison Tyler, "President John Tyler's Grandson, Harrison Tyler, on Still Being Alive" by Dan Amira from the New York *Intelligencer* January 27, 2012
10. Polk, James K. *Inaugural Address, March 4, in Polk's hand.* March 4, 1845. Manuscript/Mixed Material. https://www.loc.gov/item/pin1603/.
11. Abraham Lincoln, "Letter to Mr. Speed" written August 24, 1855 found in *The Life of Abraham Lincoln* by J. G. Holland (Springfield, MA: Gurdon Bill, 1866)
12. 48 US Code Chapter 8 § 1411
13. Jean H. Baker, *James Buchanan* (New York: Henry Holt, 2004)
14. B. H. Monroe, "Saga of Lincoln's Body" by Dorothy Meserve Kunhardt found in *Life* Magazine Vol. 54, No. 7, February 15, 1963
15. Mr. Doster, "Questioning Samuel McAllister For the Defense— May 30" found in *The Assassination of President Lincoln and the Trial of the Conspirators* compiled by Benn Pitman (Cincinnati: More, Wilstach, Baldwin, 1865)
16. Mark Twain, *Autobiography of Mark Twain* Vol. I ed. by Harriet Elinor Smith (Berkely: University of California Press: 2010)
17. Rutherford B. Hayes, "Obama's whopper about Rutherford B. Hayes and the telephone" by Glenn Kessler from The Washington *Post*, March 16, 2012
18. James A Garfield, *The Life and Public Career of Gen. James A. Garfield* by Gen. James S. Brisbin (Boston: Hubbard Bros., 1880)
19. Leon F. Czolgosz, *The Last Words if Distinguished Men and Women* by Frederic Rowland Marvin (New York: Fleming H. Revell, 1902)
20. Theodore Roosevelt, "Journal entry for Thursday, February, 14, 1884" (Library of Congress)
21. The Los Angeles *Times*, "Atlanta, Ga. January 15—[Exclusive Dispatch]" printed Saturday, January 16, 1909
22. Edith Wilson, *Edith and Woodrow* by Phyllis Lee Levin (New York: Scribner, 2001)
23. Calvin Coolidge, *The Autobiography of Calvin Coolidge* (New York: Cosmopolitan Book, 1929)

24. Franklin D. Roosevelt, "Address of the President to the Congress of the United States" Broadcast from the Capitol, Washington, D.C. December 8, 1941—12.30 pm, E.S.T. (National Archives)
25. Harry S. Truman, "Letter to Dean Acheson" November 2, 1950 https://www.shapell.org/manuscript/harry-truman-assassination-attempt/#transcripts
26. "LBJ Medal Citation" http://www.lbjlibrary.org/lyndon-baines-johnson/lbj-biography/lbj-military-service
27. Richard Nixon, "Remarks at a Reception for Returned Prisoners of War" May 24, 1973 found in *Public Papers of the Presidents of the United States Richard Nixon 1973* (Washington: United States Government Printing Office, 1975)
28. Walter Cronkite, *The Co-Presidency of Bush and Cheney* by Shirley Anne Warshaw (Stanford: Stanford University Press, 2009)
29. Jimmy Carter, "Nobel Prize Speech" December 10, 2002 https://www.nobelprize.org/prizes/peace/2002/carter/lecture/
30. Ronald Reagan, "Letter to Herman G. Rowland" [Governor Reagan] January 22, 1973 letter found at the Jelly Belly Candy Company https://www.atlasobscura.com/articles/jelly-belly-ronald-reagan
31. George H. W. Bush, "Remarks to the Supreme Soviet of the Republic of the Ukraine in Kiev, Soviet Union" August 1, 1991 found in *Public Papers of the Presidents of the United States George Bush 1991* (Washington: United States Government Printing Office, 1992)

JUNE
1. Daniel Boone, "Adventures of colonel Daniel Boon" found in *The American Museum* Vol. II (Philadelphia: Matthew Carey, 1787)
2. Robert E. Wright and David J. Cowen, *Financial Founding Fathers* (Chicago: University of Chicago Press, 2006)
3. William Clark, "Journal entry October 13, 1805" found in *Journals of the Lewis and Clark Expedition*
4. Thomas Freeman, *Southern Counterpart to Lewis & Clark* ed. by Dan Louie Flores (Norman, OK: University of Oklahoma Press, 1984)
5. "The Ballad of Davy Crockett" words by Tom Blackburn and music by George Bruns (New York: Wonderland Music Company, 1954 [copyrighted by the Walt Disney Company]) found in the University of Illnois Archives
6. Samuel Houston, "Breach of Privilege" Monday May 7, 1832 found in *Gales & Seaton's Register of Debates in Congress* Part II of Volume VIII
7. Marcus Whitman, *How Marcus Whitman Saved Oregon* by Oliver W. Nixon (Chicago: Star Publishing, 1895)
8. Geronimo, *Geronimo's Story of His Life* ed. by S. M. Barrett [told by Geronimo] (New York: Duffield, 1906)
9. "Joint Resolution For Admitting the State of Ohio into the Union" August 7, 1953 Public Law 204 Ch. 337
10. Seth Big Crow, "Crazy Horse Memorial Generates Mixed Feelings- 2003-09-12" published October 26, 2009 by *Voice of America*
11. Pat Garrett, *The Authentic Life of Billy, the Kid* (Santa Fe, NM: New Mexican Printing and Publishing, 1882)
12. Art T. Burton, *Black Gun Silver Star* (Lincoln, NE: University of Nebraska Press, 2006)
13. "Gold Spike" found in the Iris & B. Gerald Cantor Center for Visual Arts at Stanford University; Gift of David Hewes
14. Jefferson Davis, "War Department Washington, May 10, 1855" from Papers Relating to First Expedition found in *Report of the Secretary of War* (Washington: A.O.P. Nicholson, 1857)
15. Elmer McCurdy Tombstone https://www.findagrave.com/memorial/1706/elmer-mccurdy
16. Wyatt Earp, "'Sharkey Wins By a Foul Said Referee Earp'" in The San Francisco *Examiner* Thursday, December 3, 1896
17. "Ballad of Jesse James" (From Jackson County, Missouri; country whites; MS. of F. A. Brown, student in Harvard University; 1907) found in *The Journal of American Folk-lore* Vol. XXV (Lancaster, PA: American Folk-Lore Society, 1912)

18. Carry A. Nation, *The Use and Need of the Life of Carry A. Nation* (Topeka, KS: F. M. Steves & Sons, 1909)

19. "Riders Oath" found in *Heroes of the Plains* by J. W. Buel (New York: N. D. Thompson, 1882)

20. Frederick Jackson Turner, "The Significance of the Frontier in American History" found in *Proceedings of the State Historical Society, of Wisconsin* 41st annual meeting held December 14, 1893

21. Wyatt Earp, *The Gunfighter: Man or Myth?* By Joseph G. Rosa (Norman, OK: University of Oklahoma Press, 1969)

22. Allan Pinkerton, *Criminal Reminiscences and Detective Sketches* (New York: G. W. Dillingham, 1878)

23. Unknown historian, "Raising the Chicago streets out of the mud" by David Young found in the *Chicago Tribune* December 18, 2007

24. John Fraley, "Civic Doody" by Jim Mann found in *Daily Inter Lake* April 24, 2009

25. Chief Joseph, "An Indian's Views of Indian Affairs" found in *The North American Review* ed. by Allen Thorndike Rice Vol. CXXVIII (New York: D. Appleton, 1879)

26. Shufelt, S, and Lessing J. Rosenwald Reference Collection. *A letter from a gold miner, Placerville, California, October.* San Marino, Calif.: Friends of the Huntington library, 1944. Pdf. https://www.loc.gov/item/44005704/.

27. Stoudenmire-Manning treaty, *The Shooters* by Leon Claire Metz (El Paso, TX: Mangan Books, 1976)

28. David Elliott, *Last Raid of the Daltons* (Coffeyville, KS: Coffeyville Journal Print, 1892)

29. Annie Oakley, *Annie Oakley* by Shirl Kasper (Norman, OK: University of Oklahoma Press, 1992)

30. Laura Ingalls Wilder, *The Ghost in the Little House* by William Holtz (Columbia, MO: University of Missouri Press, 1993)

Made in the USA
Middletown, DE
10 June 2020